My Mother's Song

My Mother's Song

A MEMOIR

By Ellen E. Gee

My Mother's Song: A Memoir

Second Edition

Copyright © 2015 by Ellen E. Gee

All rights reserved. No part of this publication may be reproduced, stored in a retrieval system, or transmitted in any form by any means, electronic, mechanical, photocopy, recording, or otherwise, without the prior permission of the publisher, except as provided by USA copyright law.

ISBN-13: 978-1516803989
ISBN-10: 1516803981

Cover design: Jim Gibson
Printed in the United States of America

To Aunt Jeanne Marie,
the most honorable person I have ever known.

I am the picture she never painted,
The book she never wrote;
I am the symphony in her soul and
The song within her throat.

I am the pain she often suffered,
The poverty life dealt;
I am the prayer she ever uttered
To heal the hurts I felt.

— BLANCHE LANDERS

Prologue

Few of us who watched the six perfectly dressed Marines carry my mother's casket up the walkway at Quantico Cemetery ever saw the fire that once burned in her eyes. On that cold October day in 1989, most of those gathered under the small cedar hut had no idea how she could dazzle. As a kid, I'd seen it, but only a flicker, and only when she played Beethoven.

Five days before, when the phone call came from my brother Jim, I'd fumbled through the darkness, knowing it was him, knowing his words before he uttered them. "I'm sorry, Ellen. Mother died last night."

"No Jim," I wanted to say, "She really died twenty-two years ago."

I was almost eleven that day, the day the light flickered from my mother's eyes. With the pull of a trigger, the smell of smoke, the sounds of screaming.

My father lying in a widening pool of his own blood.

For years afterward, I looked for my mother in the old photos she kept tucked away. The strong Marine in her dress blues, the elegant college student dolled up for the ball, the brilliant teacher in front of her classroom.

I listened for her too. For the smooth unhurried way she spoke. The perfect way she pronounced each word. I listened for the patient way she talked me through a needlepoint stitch or how to sew on a sleeve. I even listened for the rustle of the newspapers she constantly read.

But I never recaptured the woman who'd given her life for me.

Perhaps I'd never find her, I realized, as I stood over her open grave, the sun reflecting off her baby blue casket. When I tossed in the yellow rose I'd been carrying, my sister Sheila tossed in hers.

As if to hurry us up, the backhoe's engine revved and the noise cackled over the smooth hillside, over the graves of her fellow Marines and down the road toward the iron gates at the entrance to Quantico. I stepped back as the driver shifted gears and a bucket of dirt splattered, covering my mother in a red, thick bath of Virginia clay.

A strong wind picked up and a sea of dried leaves swept across the grass, cackling like rushing water. Hundreds of blackbirds fluttered over my head, cawing to each other as they landed in the treetops, hovering, watching us grieve.

Perhaps the hardest part wasn't grieving her death.

It was watching her live.

THE DREAM

IN MEMORIES OF MY FATHER, he never speaks. Sometimes, I see him dressed in a plain white tee shirt and tan pants, sitting by the side of our house in a simple wooden chair. The sun is beating down on his weathered white skin. His head is bare, revealing a receding hairline and a small bald spot. His right leg is crossed over his left, the bottom of his trousers hiked up, exposing his skinny calf above the top of his clunky brown work boots. He's reading a book written in German.

Sometimes, my memories wander back to our small living room. He's standing there, playing the mandolin he kept hung on the wall. It looks odd the way it's pulled high on his chest like a miniature guitar. He plays with intensity, but I don't hear the music and he never sings. He just strums, his brow furrowed and his lips pulled tight, showing just a bit of his tobacco-stained teeth.

Some days, I see him in the front yard, early in the morning, raising his Confederate flag. His body is erect, his jaw tilted in deep respect as he watches it climb the pole. By the looks of him, you'd never know it'd been a hundred years since the South lost that war. To this day, I still wonder how a Yankee from Rhode Island became such a staunch Confederate.

It was thirty years after his death before I allowed a picture of him to join the photos of my family that lined the stairway to our basement. The faces of my life's story covered every wall. I spent hours there, staring at the people I loved, reliving the best moments of my life. When I decided to allow my father to enter the gallery, I tucked him into the farthest corner, out of sight from my favorite perch on the top step.

After sixteen years of marriage, my husband Tim and I were

My Mother's Song

struggling to get along. We both worked full time, and with two teenagers, I just didn't have the energy to face my father.

But a session with our therapist had jolted me. Tim and I were seated on opposite ends of the sofa when Tom handed us each a pencil and a blank sheet of paper. With a smile he said, "I want you both to draw a floor plan of the house you grew up in."

Quickly, I scribbled out each room. Tim, the meticulous carpenter, used the edge of a magazine to straighten his lines. It was lighthearted fun until Tom asked, "Now, take me through a day in the life of that house."

My heart skipped a beat, it pounded through my chest. I sucked in a gulp of air. My hands trembled and the sobs came in hiccups.

Tim, trying to console me, put his arm around my shoulder, "It's okay, honey, I'll do mine."

Then he described a charming summer day roaming the streets of Augusta, Georgia. He told of playing in the creek off Boy Scout Road. Coming home all sweaty, to his mother in the kitchen, cooking dinner.

Trying to ignore my fear, I imagined a ten-year-old Tim busting through his front door. His face covered in freckles, his crew cut damp with sweat. The smell of chili cooking on the stove. His mom's shrill voice reminding him to take off his muddy shoes.

Tim's voice hovered over my dread. Speaking softly, he made quick puzzled glances at me. I sat still, trying to calm the unknown fear erupting in my chest.

When he finished, the room fell silent, except for my sniffles.

"I'm sorry," I said. "But I can never go back in that house again."

Tenderly, Tom leaned over and took the paper off my lap. "I know, Ellen," he said. "You don't have to. I got what I needed."

But as he spoke, my mind wandered. The still simmering fear confused me. Where did it come from? After Father died, I'd gone back in that house many times. It remained vacant for years, and I helped clean it out when it finally sold. To this day, when business takes me close by, I slowly drive down the street and stare at the outside. Not once had I ever felt fear.

That day, I saw how much I denied my fear. How I spent hordes of energy trying to keep it away. How it reared its ugly head in the middle of the night. It was time, I decided, to face it down and make it stop impacting my life. It was time to put the memories of my father in their proper place.

So I added his picture to my gallery. It's strange I chose the one with him in his *lederhosen*. As a child, I hated those black suede shorts and matching suspenders. It embarrassed me when he wore them, his red tie tucked underneath the leather breastplate. But there he was, in our backyard, standing in front of the shed, holding the neck of his guitar that's propped up on a stool. His left hand is in his pocket, holding back the front of his grey *Trachten* jacket. The brim of his alpine hat is pushed back, revealing the squint embedded in his brow from years in the sun as a merchant seaman. His gray beard is closely clipped and his eyes are tense. As always, there is no smile.

Part of me thought adding him to the gallery would stop the nightmares, or at least help me make peace with him. Part of me thought his picture might spark a fond memory buried beneath the bad. Or, if nothing else, help me admit to myself that I, like my father, was a gifted writer.

Father's picture made me start to remember—what little I could recall. For the past ten years, I've passed that picture a million times as I've climbed up and down those stairs. Mostly, I avoided it, but each time it caught my eye, I stopped for a second and stared at the *lederhosen* and the guitar. I leaned in for a closer look at his face. Then I shrugged and shook my head, wondering how he ended up as my father.

But the picture didn't immediately bring back his voice. Nor did it instantly replay the soundtrack from that day. At first, all I remembered was a stream of silent images. His drunken stagger as he climbed the stairs. A locked bedroom door. Father banging, trying to get in. His gun, tucked into the belt of his trousers.

My brothers' and sisters' faces are crystal clear. James' worried look, Sheila's devastation. Brian's childish bewilderment. Nora, just five, is too young to be afraid. We're all there, but me. It's as though my eyes were binoculars, and I was far away, peering into someone else's life. Not living it—just watching it happen. The only sounds I remembered were the sirens. First the police, then the ambulance.

Even in my nightmares, my father was silent. On those rare nights when I drifted into a deep sleep, I saw him. Always the same, it's late at night and I'm running along the cobblestone streets of Old Town Alexandria. Its just stopped raining and Father is chasing me, but I don't know why. I don't hear his footsteps or his breathing; I hear only my own gasps as I struggle for air.

Looking for someplace to hide, I run down the middle of a dark narrow cobblestone road lined on both sides with seventeenth-century rowhouses. His footsteps are still silent, but I know he's following me. I sneak into the shadow of a dark porch and peek around the corner. I see him; he's poking his head into every doorway, glancing down the side streets, slowly and methodically looking for me.

The dreams always ended the same. I enter a vacant rowhouse and run from room to room, looking for a place to hide. Panting, I find safety behind a two-way mirror that looks into an interrogation room. Through the mirror, I see the doorknob turn and Father step into the room. He's wearing a long dark coat and the brim of that damn alpine hat shadows his face. Still he makes no sound.

He slowly scans the room and stops when he sees the mirror. He walks toward me and, even though he's just inches from me, I still can't see his face. I could touch him if not for the glass. His right hand comes up from his side and reaches out toward me and I'm jolted awake.

Each time, I sit up in bed unsure of where I am. Sweat beads on my forehead and my heart pounds. I'm out of breath like I really was running, panicked through the streets. Usually it takes me a few moments to realize I was dreaming. It takes a few more to realize it was "that" dream.

After my eyes adjust to the darkness, the familiarity of my bedroom helps me calm down. Then, I take inventory of my surroundings. The rhythm of my husband snoring. Our loyal cocker spaniel, asleep next to the bed. The moon shining through our wall of windows. Its pale blue shadows on our solid cherry dresser. Then I remind myself, this room is real and the dream is not.

Exhausted, I fall back on my pillow and wipe the sweat from my brow. It takes a while for my heart to slow down. It's usually an hour or two before I fall back asleep. But no matter how hard I try, I can't stop thinking about the nightmares, because I know I'll have to face my father to make them stop.

BEETHOVEN, THE MARINES, AND MOTHER

I'VE ALWAYS LOVED BEETHOVEN'S *Pathetique*. When I was a little girl, I'd lay on the rug in our tiny living room while Mother played that piece on our old upright piano. As the music flowed through our home, all the confusion that was part of my everyday life was driven away by the beauty of the music. Beethoven was her favorite composer. Usually the music was sad and she cried as she played. Her tears filled my soul as I dreamed of ways to make her life better.

The old upright piano took up half our dining room. It stood there alone, like an altar of hope, a sanctuary to absorb my grief. Around the carved flowers on the box that hid its inner workings, the dark brownish stain had cracked and begun to peel. Many of the keys were chipped, revealing the wood underneath. And the ivory had faded to a deep yellow, like the old dice Father used to play acey-ducy.

It never sounded out of tune to me. But Mother complained about it constantly. Sometimes, when she played and her fingers hit a sour note, she raised them off the keys, wrinkled her nose, and said, "Ah!" I didn't care. I lifted the lid and watched the little felt hammers dance along the tightly drawn strings.

The music was my escape, and hers too.

On the days I found her alone in the living room, I begged, "Play the piano, Mother. Pleeease."

She'd be sitting on the sofa doing needlepoint. Without looking up she'd say, "Not today, Ellen. Besides, it's horribly out of tune."

I'd pull out the bench, plop down on the edge and whine, "I don't care. I love to hear you play."

"I said not today, Ellen. I'm too tired."

"But I'll turn the pages," I would promise, swinging my feet off the edge of the bench.

Setting down her needlepoint, she'd release a long sigh and stand up. "Well, I guess. If you're going to turn the pages."

The hardwood floor creaked underneath her heavy steps. Her head hung low as she crossed the room. But when she sat down on the bench, her shoulders went back and her spine straightened. With her feet lightly hovered over the pedals and her fingers arched over the keys, she'd sit motionless for a few seconds staring at the music, as if trying to decide where she wanted to go. Then, as if a memory sparked and she made up her mind, her chin would rise slightly and her eyes begin to twinkle. She'd ruffle through the pages of sheet music, smoothing them out with the palm of her hand.

With the music selected, she'd turn to me and say, "Are you ready?" I'd shake my head yes. "Remember to watch for my nod."

Standing on her right, my fingers rested gently on the corner of the music. I'd stare at the notes and follow along as she played. The notes climbed up and down the bars as her fingers flowed up and down the keys. When the time came, she'd nod, and I would turn the page. She was so good, she never missed a beat, even if I was slow. Somewhere, in the dance between the notes on the page and my mother's fingers, all my problems would disappear.

When Mother played, I always thought she drifted to a different place. A place I didn't know and wouldn't know until I got older. Her shoulders relaxed, the muscles of her face softened, and the corners of her lips turned slightly up. A depth grew in her eyes that didn't exist in her everyday life. I'd swear she entered a world I couldn't see.

When I learned more about her, I wondered if she went back to the 1940's and Texas State College for Women. She spent four years there, summers included. Not satisfied with one major, she pursued two, music education and journalism. She was somebody there, a part of the famed rifle team who challenged the boys of Texas A&M, beating them twice.

Perhaps she remembered how news of their victory traveled around the world. How it made all the Texas papers. Maybe she remembered the headline in the *Dallas Morning News*, "Crack A&M Marksmen Lose to Girl Rifle Team."

Maybe she went back to Cherry Point, North Carolina, during WWII. As one of the first female Marines, she taught the troops there how to shoot and disassemble the Browning machine gun. In 1944, she reported to the alumni at TSCW, "I suppose it is rather a far cry from teaching music, but I teach machine guns … I was the first girl to do this work here …"

Perhaps she went back to the day a *Life* magazine photographer took her picture in front of her class. In it, he captured her exquisite profile as she stood confidently in front of twenty young Marines. The waves of her brown hair are neatly in place. The long gun and its parts are scattered across a table. She's pointing to something in her right hand. The GI's are focused in rapt attention, there is no doubt as to her expertise. When she played the piano, did she think back to the day that picture spread across the bottom of two pages of the monthly magazine?

Or maybe she remembered watching the nightly ceremonial lowering of the flag. Once, she detailed that event in a letter home to her parents. She said how rewarding her work at Cherry Point was. How it helped save men's lives, how she felt like a real Marine. "I love it here," she closed. "I am happy. I am happy to the very core of me."

I'm sure there were times when she played that she remembered being a little girl on her granny's Texas farm. "In the mornings after the rooster crowed," she once told me, "I ran barefooted to the barn and stole the morning's eggs from under the hens. You had to be quick because those big fat hens fiercely guarded their eggs." She raised her hand as if the hen was right in front of her. "I shoved my hand under the hen and grabbed the egg and pulled it out as fast as I could." Her hand jabbed out and her fingers closed as though that egg was out there in midair. "If I wasn't fast," she smiled, "those old hens pecked my arm and it hurt."

When she told me that story, I saw the beautiful little girl in all the old pictures she kept in the attic. I imagined my mother's blond ringlets my grandmother had pressed in a frame, dancing around her head as she bounded back to the house with her skirt full of eggs.

Maybe the music reminded her of hiding in the folds of her granny's skirt, listening for the whistle of the mail train making its way to town.

Once, after I was married, she took me to the old train station, which had since become a museum. It was closed that day, but as she stood on the wooden deck, peeking in the windows pointing things out, I saw the little girl in my mother's eyes.

"The train came every afternoon," she told me. "When we heard the whistle, we stopped what we were doing and started walking to the station. All the women and children on the neighboring farms came too. We gathered right there and talked and waited." She pointed inside the window to the large open area. I pressed my nose against the cool glass.

The smell of a summer rainstorm lingered in the air. A gentle breeze blew the loose strands of hair around her face. The lipstick she put on earlier had faded to a thin red line along the edge of her mouth. But her eyes danced with excitement; her head tilted as if, off in the distance, she could still hear that train's whistle blowing.

"The mail bag was unloaded and we heard the *schuut, schuut* of the postman sliding letters in the slots. When he finished, we heard the rolling door on the other side close and the click of his key locking it down. It was the sign our mail was ready."

Her hazel eyes opened wide, her brows arched with excitement. She tilted her head to one side and the corners of her mouth turned in a tender smile. "Everyone unlocked their boxes, pulled out their mail, and walked back home. It was the big social gathering of the day."

She was a grandmother that day, three times over, but I saw

a young girl. A beautiful blond spitfire full of adventure. Unafraid and eager to explore everything. Fire blazed in her eyes; the dazzle I knew once existed. I soaked it all in, wondering how things went so wrong.

But on those days when I watched my mother play the piano, all these images of her were just stories in my head. Once in a while I pulled out the *Life* magazine and stared at the picture of the beautiful intelligent woman. I opened the box of old photos and marveled at my favorite. The one of her in uniform, standing next to a Browning machine gun that's mounted on a tripod. Both her hands are firmly grasping its handles. Her smile is wide, her cheeks pushed all the way to her eyes. I never saw my mother look so happy.

But those women were not my mother. The woman sitting beside me at the piano was overweight. Most of the time her eyes were tired and her shoulders drooped. She no longer bothered to curl her hair and she rarely found time to play the piano. By the time I began to wonder who my mother really was, those other parts of her no longer existed.

BUCHANAN STREET

IN 1957, WHEN I WAS EIGHT MONTHS old, my parents bought one of the thirty two-story duplexes that lined both sides of South Buchanan Street in Arlington, Virginia. From the beginning to the cul-de-sac at the end, each unit sat the same distance from the road and the same distance from each other. On all the streets around us, every house was different, but on Buchanan Street, every home was exactly the same.

In the late fifties, Arlington's population had exploded. With the Pentagon and downtown DC just minutes away, people came from all over the country for government jobs. On Buchanan Street, young parents of large families packed into the small houses as a stepping-stone to larger homes in the sprawling outer suburbs. Too many people in too small a space forced the kids outdoors.

In the summer, despite the sweltering heat, our great diversions were ball games like kickball, spud, and pickle. Usually they started in the street with two kids tossing a ball and grew into a mob of 20 or 30 — so many sometimes that only the bigger ones played while us younger siblings sat to the side waiting to take someone's place.

Now it's hard to believe that running, shouting, and tagging were good for so many hours of entertainment, but when Mother flicked the "come home" porch light, or we heard the bell from the Hockaday's house down the street, none of us wanted to stop. We each began to calculate how many signs we could ignore and still get away with claiming we didn't see or hear them. But when my father came out and blew his boatswain mate's whistle, we Gibson's knew not to mess around. We dropped everything and ran for home.

My Mother's Song

As a kid, the sameness of the houses on Buchanan Street made me want to fit in. I wanted my father to be young and handsome like most of the other dads. I wanted him to wear dark suits with skinny ties, and not that goofy looking bow tie and burgundy blazer. I wanted to call my parents "Mom" and "Dad." But I didn't dare. We were supposed to be sophisticated, so only *Mother* and *Father* would do.

Father's tattoo's embarrassed me the most. None of the other father's had any. But my father had chains around both his wrists, anchors woven with ivy on his biceps, both arms, top and bottom, were covered with nautical stars. I always wanted the one that said "Mother" to be a tribute to my own mother. Father said he got them in Taiwan, long before he met her, so I knew it honored the grandmother I never met.

During the sixties, big Chevy's and Buick's sat parked like shiny trophies in our neighbors' driveways. To my recollection, we owned the only foreign car on the street, a light bluish-green VW Bug. Father said the "people's wagon" represented the genius of his German heritage. Its design was perfect for our clan of eight. On family outings, Nora and Brian scrunched into the small cubbyhole in what we called the "way back," while the remaining four of us squeezed onto the back seat. What did we need one of those big American cars for? It worked okay, I guess, until we all began to grow.

In 1963, my grandfather Rice retired as Vice President and Secretary of the Board of the Dallas Federal Reserve Bank. Before he cleaned out his desk, the State Department commissioned him as an advisor to the Nigerian Central Bank. To prepare for the two-year tour, mother's parents moved into an apartment in DC, not far from where we lived. Horrified to see his daughter and grandchildren packed into the bug, my grandfather bought Mother a brand new VW Bus. When she pulled it into our driveway I cringed. I'd never seen anything so odd looking. Secretly, I longed for a Chevy Impala just like the brand new one parked next door in Mr. Rouse's driveway.

Without the invention of air-conditioning, all summer long every window on Buchanan Street stood wide open. Not even the whirl of our big box fans blocked the indoor sounds from drifting outside. Gentle conversations and the faint chatter of televisions wafted out into the middle of the street. From the sidewalk you could even hear forks and knives scraping across china.

At eight o'clock on Sunday nights, the theme song for *Walt Disney's Wonderful World of Color* flowed in stereo out most windows. Not ours though, Father refused to buy us an "idiot box." But most of the kids who had wandered back outside after dinner heard it and hurried home. The chirpy theme song tugged at my heart, reminding me of my broken family.

Left alone in front of our house, with my body sticky from the humid summer air, I would shuffle my feet, hoping to prod the Rouse's to invite me in to watch the show. Sometimes, through their open screen door, I watched Tinker Bell swoop over Cinderella's Castle, tip her wand, and sprinkle fairy dust on everyone below. When they did ask me in, I envied their neatly decorated living room. The way Mr. and Mrs. Rouse sat close to each other on the sofa. How Ginger and her little brother spread out on their stomachs in front of the TV. How Mr. Rouse spoke gently to his wife and children. The peace and quiet of their home sprinkled over me like a soft evening rain after a long hot day of playing ball.

On those steamy nights, I walked up and down our street listening as the upbeat TV shows floated out the windows. Their constant laugh tracks made me feel like everyone was having fun but me. Because if you stood in front of 1202 South Buchanan Street, you didn't hear laughter. What you heard was my father reading out loud in German. Or maybe him strumming on his guitar or mandolin. On Mondays, Wednesdays, and Fridays, you heard him teaching James and Alfred how to use a slide rule.

Some nights, with the windows wide open, my father, in his thick New England accent, could be heard recording his rants against the blacks, President Kennedy, and the Jews. Into the microphone of his blue reel-to-reel tape player, he said they were the enemy, that we must prepare for war, for the invasion of our neighborhoods. Some days, he would drive around Arlington blasting the tapes from a speaker in our car.

Once, in the middle of the night, he thought the war had started. Asleep in the living room on the pullout sofa, Father thought someone had entered the house. Still drunk from an earlier visit to the VFW hall, he grabbed the loaded pistol he kept by his bed. He fired six wild shots toward the kitchen door.

The shots woke me from a deep sleep. I struggled to understand what the noise had been. Mother ran out of her room and down the stairs yelling, "For Pete's sake Edmund, what are you thinking?" Afraid to leave my room, I walked to the window. Our neighbors, the Uhler's, back porch light came on. Mr. Uhler came rushing out his door shouting at his wife to stay inside. I heard our back door open and the screen door slam. Mr. Uhler threw up his arms and shouted across the yard, "One of these days you're going to kill someone." A month later, the Uhlers moved away.

Three bullets were embedded in the kitchen doorframe. Another one hit the binding of the Fannie Farmer Cookbook on the shelf in the dining room. Its path formed a two-inch channel through the pages, pushing the paper back like little accordions. We still used it by smoothing out the tight folds with the back of our fingernails.

The more Father talked about war, the more paranoid he became about our safety. In 1961, for Sheila's protection, he held her back from starting school until the following year, putting us in the same grade. During the summer, he made the four of us, Alfred, James, Sheila and me, practice walking to school in what he called "formation." Like little storm troopers, he lined us up on the sidewalk with James and Alfred in the front and Sheila and me in step right behind them.

But a week before school started, a fight broke out in our

front yard. An older kid said something about Father I didn't understand. Before I knew what happened, a shovel had ripped a gash in my left heel. Sitting next to father in the boiling heat of the emergency room, my palms sweat around the fifty-cent piece he gave me earlier for "silver medicine." But, I sensed a shift in my world. Father sat with his legs crossed staring straight ahead. His lips were pulled tight and he repeatedly smoothed his moustache and beard with his long fingers. My stomach prickled with a gut feeling my life was drastically changed. But I didn't know why.

Within a week, a six-foot redwood plank fence went up from the front edge of our house all around the side and backyard. The workers sawed off each plank at a forty-five degree angle, then nailed them up with just enough room in between for the neighborhood kids to peer in on us. In the corner of the front yard, Father mounted a tall flagpole for the Confederate flag that usually hung on the pole over our front window. When it was all done, our house look exactly like a fort from the Civil War.

My rage against Father boiled when he told us we could no longer play outside the fence. To make it worse, he dug up the grass and covered the yard with tan pea gravel. Then he built a wooden platform for a boxing ring and enclosed it with rope.

Every Saturday, Father made Alfred and James "work out." Early in the morning, dressed up in their baggy satin Everlast shorts, Father laced up their big fat red mittens. Acting like the referee, he danced around my brothers, prodding them to fight. Alfred didn't flinch as he took jab after jab at James. James kept his gloves over his face and struggled to return Alfred's blows. Most mornings, James left the ring with a bloody nose.

Our neighbors complained about our fortress until a county inspector showed up and paced the sidewalk in front of our house. That afternoon, I had the perfect view from our picture window when Father's bug barreled into our driveway. Red faced with his eyes raging, he stood in the front yard, a few inches from the inspector's face. The poor guy stood there patiently but never backed down. For days Father raged on and on about the "communist" government taking over America.

But he lost that war. The fence around the side yard was cut down to three feet. Since it couldn't protect us from the evil people stalking the neighborhood, Father banned the Gibson kids from the side yard. Leaving us confined in the small backyard with the boxing ring.

It didn't take long for the fence to feel like the lid of a shaken coke bottle. With the six of us kids trapped inside like spinning tops agitating the gasses. Anything that caused a slight lift of the edge released an erupting hiss.

Mother tried to divert our attention with puzzles and games, but we fought constantly over space. With no place to run, our energy exploded on each other.

I suppose the fence did keep us safe from the neighbors. But I was never afraid of them. The odd thing was, my biggest fears were always right there, inside my own house.

MARTIN LUTHER KING AND FATHER

IN JULY 1963, I TURNED SEVEN. By then, I knew my father hated people like *kikes, Jews* and *niggers,* but I had no idea how his hatred would end up affecting me. I just thought he hated everyone except his friend, Mrs. Lane. And since I didn't like her, I figured Father was wrong about all those other people too.

I couldn't tell you why I didn't like Mrs. Lane. It just annoyed me the way she seemed to hover on the outskirts of our lives. How she showed up at public events as if she knew Father would be there. She was pleasant, but her manners seemed forced, like an act she performed to impress us. Mother never said she didn't like Mrs. Lane, but she never gave her the attention she did her own friends.

Earlier that same summer, Father built a small shed in our backyard. It looked like a miniature house with redwood siding, a shingled roof, and a front door that was two feet off the ground. He placed it on sturdy legs and nailed a few extra runs of siding along the bottom. At first I thought it was cute, like a playhouse. That's what I wanted it to be. Since we were not allowed outside our fence, it only seemed right that Father build something for us to play in. That's what the other fathers would have done.

After he finished the shed, I waited for Father to leave it unlocked. He'd talked about a hidden compartment under the floor, and I was dying to see what was in it. I still hoped, in some way, the shed was for us. The hidden compartment could be a secret place to hide my toys where Brian and Nora couldn't find them. Maybe Father would let Sheila and me play house inside the shed. She'd be the mother, and I'd grab my briefcase and slam the door on my way to "work." There seemed no end to the fun I could have in the shed.

One Saturday, weeks later, Father took some tools out and I followed him to the upstairs bedroom, where he was installing a shelf. Figuring he'd be there a while, I slipped away and went back to the shed. To my delight, he had left the front door wide open, as if inviting me to come inside.

At first, I didn't go in. I stood by the door, scraping away gravel with my foot until I had a small circle of bare dirt. I peeked inside and looked around. On the floor, just inside the door, a couple boxes of screws and the hand plane Father used to smooth the edges of his shelf lay on sticky black tar paper scored with light yellow lines.

One more time, I scouted out the yard before climbing inside. With my sneakers sticking to the tarpaper, I pushed the hardware and the plane off to the side and peeled back the paper. There was the plywood trap door with a rope handle tucked into the wood. With both hands, I lifted the heavy door. There, lying in their own bed, were four rifles. Like everything Father did, they were perfectly lined up, their oily light-brown stocks at one end and their narrow greasy barrels at the other. Their triggers pointed up.

Staring at the rifles, I froze. My stomach twisted, and my nose tinged at their greasy smell. The cute aura of the shed disappeared and I dropped the lid. I jumped out the door and ran back upstairs to check on Father. When I walked into the room, he glanced over at me, then went back to putting the finishing touches on the shelf.

I sat on the floor and thought of *all* his guns. His favorite, the one he called the Luger, when not in the holster under his jacket, sat loaded on the table next to his bed. There was the small .22 he called a "woman's gun," that he made Mother carry in her purse. He had one with a barrel that twirled, but I'd only seen it a few times. And now the four rifles hidden in the shed.

By early afternoon, Father had finished the shelf and put the tools neatly back. Sheila and I were kicking around in the backyard when he shut the door and snapped the padlock together. In an unusually good mood he said, "Come on, girls, I'd like to go show you off." Meaning he was going somewhere and we were invited along.

Since Sheila was his recent favorite, his "first mate," I didn't try for the front seat of his old blue VW bug. Stepping on the hand brake, I squeezed my skinny body between the two front seats and plopped down on the back seat. Father lit a cigarette and, with it dangling in his mouth, he turned around to back out. One corner of his lips parted and a cloud of smoke blew over my head. For the next few minutes, it filled the back of the car and tickled my nose.

We hadn't gone far before I realized we were headed for Old Town Alexandria. I crossed my fingers, hoping for Scotland House, the store where Father bought his kilts and *lederhosen*. Father knew the ladies there, so they were extra nice to us. They went on and on about Sheila's bright red hair. It was one of the few places where Father smiled.

As we passed the train tracks and the dilapidated row houses that lined Duke Street, Father cursed the fat black women who sat on their porches, watching their kids play.

"Lazy niggers," he said. "We should send them all back to Africa."

I let out a sigh so hard it blew my bangs off my forehead. Why couldn't he talk about something else besides black people? He didn't even know them.

It was one of those summer days when the wind didn't blow, trapping the heat and humidity close to the ground. Sitting on the edge of the backseat, I shoved my face between Sheila's head and the open window. I wrapped my fingers around her long red hair and twisted it in a knot to keep it out of my face.

On the outside of the rowhouses, large chunks of paint hung off the clapboard siding in long thick strips. The small patches of yard had little tufts of grass shooting up between large sections of reddish-brown dirt. Men and women walked past piles of trash as if it was invisible.

Most of the homes didn't have air conditioners, so the front doors stood wide open. Always curious about how black people lived, I strained my eyes to see past the women and inside their houses. When Father stopped, and I had time to let my eyes adjust to the darkness, it shocked me how the neatness of the houses' insides contrasted with the rundown outsides. Our house was the opposite—neat outside, but cluttered inside.

The road ran so close to the homes, I could look the women in the eyes as we drove by. Beads of sweat glistened off their black skin. Their hair poofed up around their heads like it wasn't even attached. They talked loudly and ran after their children, much like Mother and our neighbors did on Buchanan Street.

Father's view of them disturbed me. Even as a kid, I wondered why he hated them for something they couldn't help. And why he didn't see we'd done nothing to make ourselves white? The way he wanted to get rid of them made me want *him* to go away.

When we drove past Route 1 and Father didn't turn on the main road with all the pretty shops, my fingers uncrossed and my stomach twisted. I knew we were going to the gun shop.

The car bumped along the jutting cobblestones. We drove past the rows of old shops that had been boarded up for years. I let out a low hum so the vibration in my throat could distract me from thinking about the gun shop at the end of the street facing the river.

A tiny sign on the outside of the large warehouse said Interarms. Every time I saw the name it made me think of how we played Red Rover. Two long rows of kids with their arms linked together. I never knew what guns had to do with interlocked arms.

Father whistled as we headed for the small door leading into the warehouse. Inside the building, the lights streaming from high on the ceiling barely made it to the ground. Just inside the door stood a long glass showcase filled with rows of guns. Several men gathered around the counter, their cigarette smoke swirling around their heads. They stopped talking when we walked in.

With great pride, Father "showed us off," then waved the back of his hand for us to run on. Glad to be free of him, Sheila and I headed for the back of the building. The conversation changed to black people and President Kennedy. Their words fading the further we got away. But off in the distance I heard Father talking about "Martin Luther Coon."

My nose got used to the odd smell of rotting wood and gun grease. We ran up and down the rows of tall shelves. Each one was packed floor to ceiling with guns, some in brown boxes and some in wooden crates. On the back wall, a rolling ladder ran across a rail high over my head. Sheila and I took turns hiding behind piles of machine guns, jumping out, trying to scare each other.

When Father called us, I was glad to leave. The crowd of men hadn't left the counter, their faces still surrounded with smoke. He opened the door and a flood of sunlight came in. Outside, the hot summer air felt cool compared to the stale air of the building.

All summer long Father obsessed over the upcoming March on Washington. "Martin Luther Coon" and his "army" were coming to town and it was "going to be a war." Everyone else would be caught off guard, but not our father. He was smarter, he would be ready.

At seven, I knew enough to be afraid.

Then, one Saturday, the rifles came out of their hiding place. Father leaned them against the wall in the upstairs bedroom along the windows facing the street. He brought the green army ammo boxes up and laid them next to the rifles. He removed the screens from the windows.

Early in the morning, I wandered upstairs to the front bedroom, where Father was kneeling on the floor. When he saw me, he pointed at the first rifle and said, "This is James's rifle. He will shoot from here. You will be his ammo runner. When he runs out of bullets you will get him more."

On the floor next to him sat his transistor radio. It wasn't playing any music, just a man speaking on and on about some people gathering in the city. He said buses were unloading hundreds of people, of all races. Father mumbled under his breath, "This is the real goddamn deal. It's war this time. They're not messing around." Father's words confused me. The man on the radio didn't sound afraid, and he never said anything about a war.

Father leaned out the window and pointed up the street towards George Mason Drive.

"They'll be coming from there," he said.

I looked up and down the street. The neighborhood was strangely quiet. No kids played outside, and nobody seemed to be coming and going. I sensed something was going on, but it didn't feel scary like a war.

Again, I leaned out the window and looked towards George Mason Drive. I tried to imagine the place we skated and played kickball full of black people. I imagined them with sticks and rocks – hundreds of them – coming down the street to attack us.

Father's eyes were crazy, not with fear, but with excitement. He lit one of his unfiltered Camels, sucked in a long draw and then spit bits of tobacco off the tip of his tongue. Slowly, like a raging bull in a comic book, a steady stream of smoke came out both his nostrils. I stood back from him, afraid of getting in his way.

All day, Father fiddled around in that room. The men on the radio rambled on and on. Now they talked about the well-dressed, polite people coming by the thousands. I asked if I could go outside. There were no kids playing, but I figured I could skate.

Father said no.

Early Sunday morning, Father came in our room and woke us up.

"Come on, girls," he ordered. "It's time to give you the battle plan." Then he walked out and shut the door while Sheila and I got dressed. He was still in the hallway when we opened the door. Alfred stood next to him, bright-eyed and ready for the day. James stood behind Alfred, his eyes weary with a longing for more sleep.

In the kitchen, Father leaned against the refrigerator while we poured our cereal and milk. His white tee shirt was tucked into his khakis and cinched tight with the matching web belt he wore in the Navy. Every few minutes he checked his wristwatch as if we were running late for a show. Sensing his impatience, I ate faster.

We rinsed our bowls and gathered around Father, waiting for our instructions. Sheila finished last and when she joined the group, Father led us like little soldiers up the stairs to the front bedroom. The rifles were still lined along the open window. Static from the radio crackled in the corner.

Like a commander-in-chief, Father began to give us our positions.

"Alfred, here's your rifle. Pick it up."

Alfred, who was thirteen, reached past me and picked up the large gun like a pro and placed it against his shoulder.

"Aim it up the street," Father ordered.

Alfred pointed the gun out the window, tilted his head, closed one eye, and squinted down the barrel.

Then Father demanded James do the same.

James, who could never hurt anyone, seemed torn between following Father's orders and figuring how to talk him out of his plan. Slowly, he reached past me and picked up his rifle. The oily smell of gun grease waved past my nose. James, only ten, placed the gun to his shoulder and stretched his short arm for the trigger. He mimicked Alfred's stance, but he didn't lean out the window and when he aimed, he didn't squint. I was convinced he would never shoot.

Father became impatient, hurriedly barking off our instructions. The enemy was coming and we weren't ready. His eyes couldn't stay focused on one thing. They darted out the window, up the street and around the room, as if the enemy could be coming from anywhere.

"Sheila, you're Alfred's ammo runner," he said, pointing to one of the green army boxes. "This is your ammo. Watch him closely. When he runs out, you get him more."

Nothing Father said made sense, but Sheila, just eight, obediently nodded, crossed her legs, and plopped down on the floor next to her box of ammo.

"Ellen, you're James's ammo runner. Here's your box," he said, pointing at the green box next to James. I was glad I had James and not Alfred. I felt safer with James.

I followed Sheila's lead and sat down next to my box.

The man on the radio still talked about the buses, saying now there were thousands and thousands of people. He repeated how well dressed they were and how they were of all different races.

Nobody was on Buchanan Street and nobody was outside playing. I longed to escape the baking heat in the upstairs bedroom. My sun suit stuck to my back and beads of sweat dripped down my stomach. Anger burned inside me at Father for making me sit in front of the window. If he would just let me go outside, I could get the other kids to come out and play.

To ease my boredom, I tried to focus on the radio. I tried to imagine the scene the man described. From the tiny speakers, a crowd of people started to sing.

"We shall overcome, we shall overcome ... "

We were in our places, afraid to move; Father crouching down close to the radio, Alfred and James kneeling next to their rifles. Sheila and I sitting cross-legged next to our little green boxes.

The air in the room never changed. The afternoon dragged on. On the radio, men gave speeches, saying things I didn't understand. When the speakers got excited, the people in the crowd clapped and yelled. Their excitement set off Father's rage, filling his eyes with hate. He stood up and paced, drew his lips in tight, and squinted hard, pressing wrinkles deep into his forehead. "President Kennedy and his goddamn coon army," he cursed.

Late in the afternoon, someone introduced Martin Luther King. The first name I recognized.

"I am happy to join with you today in what will go down in history as the greatest demonstration for freedom in the history of our nation."

He didn't sound stupid the way Father described him. His voice was direct, but not angry like my father's.

The applause faded. Outside, Buchanan Street remained silent. Inside, nobody moved. We kept our positions. I looked up at Father. His eyes were wild, his brow tight.

Over the radio, Dr. King's voice remained steady.

"We must not allow our creative protest to degenerate into physical violence. Again and again, we must rise to the majestic heights of meeting physical force with soul force."

Father paced in front of the window, attempting to pump us up for the war. But Martin Luther King's voice on the radio still didn't sound angry. I thought he sounded like a preacher. He sounded nicer than my father.

"Remember, stay focused! Keep watching up the street! We will fight them off!" Father's voice boomed, like he was on a stage and not in the small area of the bedroom. I wanted to go find mother, but I was too afraid to leave the window.

Dr. King's voice continued, seeming to take over Father's. "And so, even though we face the difficulties of today and tomorrow, I still have a dream. It is a dream deeply rooted in the American dream."

I leaned out the window and looked up the street; there was nobody around. Inside, Sheila still sat on the floor next to her ammo. Alfred still seemed eager to please father. James looked worried.

I kept listening to the radio. Dr. King's powerful voice never changed, never got angry, and he still sounded like a preacher.

"And this will be the day—this will be the day when all of God's children will be able to sing with new meaning:

'My country 'tis of thee, sweet land of liberty, of thee I sing.
Land where my fathers died, land of the Pilgrim's pride,
From every mountainside, let freedom ring!'"

I became restless. I wanted to leave the window and go play. I wanted all the kids to come out and start a game of kickball. I wanted Father to put the guns back in their hiding place.

Dr. King, his voice now booming, ended his speech, nearly drowned out by the crowd's clapping. "And when this happens, when we allow freedom to ring, when we let it ring from every village and every hamlet, from every state and every city, we will be able to speed up that day when all of God's children, black men and white men, Jews and Gentiles, Protestants and Catholics, will be able to join hands and sing in the words of the old Negro spiritual:

'Free at last! Free at last!
Thank God Almighty, we are free at last!'"

The crowd roared. Dr. King's voice stopped and Father jumped up.

"Be ready, they're going to start coming. Alfred, James, pick up your guns. Girls, you be ready. If one of your brothers falls, you'll have to take over. Just grab the rifle and aim it up the street. Just fire into the crowd."

I was confused. The man on the radio kept talking about the polite, well-dressed crowd. How Dr. King gave a powerful speech. No one on the radio seemed worried about a war. But in our bedroom, nothing changed. We still sat, wide-eyed, staring out the window, looking toward George Mason Drive. We kept waiting for the enemy to come marching down the street. We waited all afternoon for an invasion of my father's making.

But nobody came. Not one single person showed up for Father's war. When the sun began to set, Father seemed disappointed. It had been hours since the speeches ended, but we were still in front of the windows, afraid to move. The radio crackled in the corner, the men quietly talked about Dr. King and how peaceful the crowd remained. They still talked about the well-dressed people from every race.

All day, I had a feeling Father was wrong. I knew hundreds of black people were not going to invade our street. I was relieved when he told us we could leave the windows.

That night I went to bed angry.

Angry at Father for making me miss a perfect day for playing kickball.

Angry at him for being crazy.

SOMEONE FINALLY GETS THE BASTARD

THERE WAS SO MUCH TO BE AFRAID of in the summer of '63. Unbeknownst to me, the country was turning upside down. As the state of Virginia began to lose its fight against integration, Father believed most citizens, like him, still wanted the schools segregated. Since 1958, he'd used his considerable skill as a writer to voice his opinions to the editors of all the newspapers around town. *The Washington Post,* the *Virginia Standard,* and the *Northern Virginia Sun* boldly published his venom, putting our family out in front of one the country's ugliest battles. Each time he was "published," he bought extra copies and clipped the letters out, saving them in a file like little badges of honor.

I was unaware of the target my Father stamped on our backs. I had no idea that damn confederate flag he flew every day was a bulls-eye for our family. Nor did I know about the arrows coming over the phone. The death threats against all us Gibsons, even down to the littlest kid. But Father viewed them as prizes. He even recorded them, playing them back to anyone who'd listen. Over and over he listened to the slimy men like him, who took their anger out on the innocent. "Dis is what I gonna do to yo' wife and kids. I's gonna cut dem to pi'ces and spread dem all ovah Ahlington."

Losing one of us for the cause didn't seem to bother him. "This is war, goddammit, and sacrifices have to be made." Someone had to protect our children from the threat of "mongrelization." And he would be that "someone." So what if they closed a few schools. We already had the supplies we needed to be homeschooled.

That is, if we stayed alive.

Without an "idiot box," I'm not left with many visual images from that summer. Of the steady news items that came over the radio, most didn't stick. Probably because what they described I couldn't imagine: fires set in cities, crowds of black people hosed off like a blaze, rows and rows of police in riot gear. How, when you are a second grader, do you put a picture to a verbal description of someone bombing a church with little girls inside? How do you grasp a voice describing how they are going to tear you limb from limb?

We had lots of newspapers, but I had just learned to read, and *The Washington Post* didn't have that chirpy "I Can Read" sticker on the front. So without the visual images of television, and with my inability to conjure up images described over the radio, my memories are limited to my immediate surroundings. I'm sure stories about Birmingham, Stratford Middle School, and Senator Byrd were discussed between the tracks of classical music on the radio. But until the March on Washington, I knew nothing about the fear outside our door, and I never connected our fence to Father's war.

At my young age, I wasn't expected to grasp the news, and fortunately I never knew what the neighbors said about my family. Nor the conversations teachers shared as we Gibson's were shuttled up the grades at Claremont Elementary. It didn't even dawn on me how much our neighbors, the Rouses, heard through the walls of our shared duplex. At the time, I somehow figured nobody knew or suspected a thing.

Every day, I went about my business oblivious to the world around me. Every day that summer, Mother dropped us off at Claremont Elementary for what we called "summer recreation." Eighty elementary school kids gathered in the back while their parents went to work. All day, I chose between games of kickball, soccer, or simple craft projects. It was a full-day recess, a refugee camp for the Gibson kids. It gave us a break from the madness we were living. Every afternoon, it tore me in two when Mother appeared around the corner of the building. Part of me was glad to see her, but part of me never wanted to go back home.

August turned to fall and school replaced "recreation." September didn't cool things off, but the school's air conditioning provided a welcome relief. At home, as always, the big box fan in front of the back screen door hummed day and night as it struggled to bring fresh air inside.

That fall, the country was changing and so was my family.

After the March on Washington, Father's rage against President Kennedy kicked into high gear. He placed a picture of him on his desk and walked back and forth in front of it shoving a thumb-down fist in his face. A sea of superlatives that were unknown to my vocabulary spewed out his mouth. He could have said anything—called him "good" and "righteous"—I wouldn't have known. But the hatred dripping in his voice sent chills up my spine.

One Saturday afternoon, I was sprawled out on the living room rug reading my new Laura Ingalls Wilder book, when the kitchen door swung open. It banged against the bookcase, and Father charged through carrying his new "target." Out of a thin piece of wood, he'd crudely cut the silhouette of a man's head and shoulders.

"We'll just call him Kennedy," he said sarcastically. "Come on fellows. Let's go for a ride."

Carrying "Kennedy," he and the boys loaded up in the VW bug, and I returned to Pa and Laura solving yet another problem on the prairie. Hours slipped by as I imagined life with a father like Pa. So far, my day had been perfect, but that changed when the car doors slammed.

After the day of "Father's War," I'd become a master at reading James's eyes. If they were light and bouncy, James was going to lead us into something fun. If they were sad, I needed to be careful and keep my mouth shut. If they were afraid, I should be too.

When Alfred came through the front door, he seemed like his normal self. But when James walked in behind him, his eyes darted quickly around the room, as if noting the whereabouts of each person. His urgency made me sit up straight, almost dropping my book. Even from across the room, I sensed his fear. Father, not far behind him, came in carrying "Kennedy." Only now, "Kennedy" had a chest full of bullet holes. I tried to make sense of it all. But what can a kid think when her father sashays in the front door, home from taking his sons shooting, with the President of the United States as their target?

Nothing in my experience had prepared me to connect the rifles in the window, Martin Luther King, and the torso of President Kennedy riddled with bullet holes. My mind couldn't process a straight thought on all those events. Even on that day, I didn't realize I was afraid, but I knew James was.

As fall slid into winter, school became a welcomed distraction. The brightness of the building with its artwork-lined halls, and the buzz of cheerful voices changed me, but only when I was there. The library became a place to dream. Sitting in the large square room, staring out the three walls of solid windows, my mind took me anyplace but where I was. Curious George, Alice in Wonderland, and the lone eye of Cyclops watched over me from their paintings high above the windows. Walking up and down the aisles, I chose books with the ability to launch me on my journeys. The librarian became my special friend.

At school, there was no pressure to "read" others' faces. No need to evaluate someone else's body language to learn what was going on. The sameness of each day allowed me to unwind. It began slowly in the mornings at the front entrance, where hundreds of kids waited for the principal to unlock the doors. Then it picked up speed as we charged in like a bunch of horses released from a corral, banging into each other while teachers reminded us to slow down. Then the peace and quiet overtook me as we sorted ourselves through the classroom doors.

When the bell rang at the end of each day, Sheila and I waited at the front doors for Alfred and James. Then we joined the sea of kids who marched down the steep hill on Columbus Street before we turned the corner and sorted ourselves to our homes.

Life as I knew it continued.

And then one Friday in November, someone really did shoot the president.

My second-grade class was taking a test. The silence invaded by the occasional sound of someone's eraser, then the hand rubbing across the page, brushing off the little rubber hairs. Mrs. Shuford sat behind her desk grading papers, making as little noise as possible when she turned a page. The principal opened the door and motioned for her to come into the hall. I looked up at the wall clock, and for a moment you could hear the red second hand tapping across the dashes. I went back to my test but looked up when Mrs. Shuford reentered the room, crying. She stood a few minutes in front of the class, struggling for the right words to say. It was as if she had said "freeze" and every kid stopped, with pencils in hand, and stared straight at her. She found her voice and her chin quivered. She told us to close our books and gather our things. We were going home.

When she said the president had been shot, I thought of Father's target and how he called it "Kennedy." Now, Mrs. Shuford was crying real hard. We barely made a sound when we pulled books out of our desks. Not a single kid talked as other teachers came in and out of the room. They cried too and hugged each other.

Kids poured out of the classrooms and quietly filled the halls. Hardly anyone spoke as we all left the building. Sheila and I found James by the front doors. Like Mrs. Shuford, he'd been crying, but he didn't say a word, maybe because there was nothing to say. Like zombies, hundreds of kids, who usually could be heard from blocks away, walked down the hill on Columbus Street in complete silence. I swear, not even the blackbirds cawed in the treetops behind the houses.

When we walked through our front door, things got confusing. We found Father in the living room in front of the picture of President Kennedy, jumping up and down. He kept saying, "Hip, hip, hooray! Hip, hip, hooray! Someone finally got the bastard!"

It felt so odd. If I opened our front door and stood on our porch, a weird sort of sadness pervaded over the neighborhood. But if I shut the door and stood in our living room, festivities filled the room. It was like I'd entered one of those cartoons where the guy opens the door to a crowd of noisy people, then he closes it and there's silence. Open, noise. Close, silence. Except it was the other way around.

All weekend Father could not contain his enthusiasm. He could not stop rejoicing over the assassination of the president. It was the happiest I'd ever seen him. All day the radio rattled with the somber news of the shooting. No music or commercials, just talk about the assassination. The newscasters choked on their words, they struggled to hold back tears. But not my father. It was like the clock struck midnight and a new year had dawned. He did everything except sing "Olde Lang Syne."

All weekend, Buchanan Street grieved. Everyone stayed indoors; no kids played kickball or any other games. My two worlds competed with each other, separated only by our front door. All day, I opened the door and stood on the front porch, then I went inside and stood in the living room. Sadness, glee. Sadness, glee.

By Monday, the mood on Buchanan Street had not changed. School was cancelled and Father started to settle down, but he was not the least bit sad. The radio blared through the living room, describing every detail of the president's funeral. Mrs. Kennedy leaving the Capital. The casket drawn by horses across Memorial Bridge. Hundreds of people lining the roadway. When a band started playing the funeral song, I couldn't stop singing the words in my head, "Pray for the dead and the dead will pray for you."

Then we heard the jets, lots of them. We heard them way off in the distance. Father jumped up and I followed him to the front porch. To my amazement, all our neighbors stood on their front porches too. For several minutes, a sea of jets flew just above the treetops at the end of the street. They rumbled past and the noise died down. Then, as if on cue, all at the same time, every neighbor went back in their house. It was the strangest thing I'd ever seen.

As far as I could tell, my father was the only person happy about President Kennedy's assassination. The shooting became a bizarre confirmation he might win the war. But I didn't know what to feel. After that day in front of the bedroom window, I didn't trust anything Father said or did. He had lots of guns and now I knew he wasn't afraid to use them. He wasn't afraid of killing another man. It was just who he was I guess, a devoted soldier in a war of his own making.

About this time, a new fear began to rise inside me. One that said I'd never grow up. I didn't recognize it at first. I only knew I looked enviously on anyone who'd lived long enough to experience a life of their own. To me, childhood became something to survive, and the freedom of adulthood, the prize for getting there.

THE SUMMER OF '65

IN THE SUMMER OF '65, Father's civilian job writing textbooks for the Navy paid well, earning him enough for us to live comfortably. But he had other plans for his money. Of course, our needs—clothing, food, medical bills—weren't added into the equation. So, to ease the financial burden, Mother went to work as a Detail Clerk with the *Northern Virginia Sun*. Though she earned far less than he, Father split the bills down the middle and forced Mother to pay half. While we peeled the masking tape price tags off our thrift store clothes, Father treated himself to imported *lederhosen* and a handmade kilt.

The day he brought his new clothes home, he spent all afternoon getting dressed. Wearing the kilt with a white shirt, he knotted a tie made of the same plaid. Ignoring the summer heat, he pulled a thick pair of wool knee socks over his hairy calves, securing them at the top with elastic rings with little red flags sticking out. Standing in front of the bathroom mirror, he adjusted and readjusted the drape of his black beret until the red pom-pom on top sat in the exact middle of his head.

When he walked past me in the living room with a thick tan jacket over his arm, a combination of sweat and wool blew by. Mother followed him carrying the new box camera my grandfather bought her on his recent trip to Hong Kong.

To my horror, they marched out to the side yard where Father buckled a little purse with tassels, the only part of his outfit I liked, around his waist. Standing next to the fence, with the sun beaming down, Father turned slightly to the side, pulled back the front of his jacket and placed his left hand on his hip. In a cold stare, he glared at Mother without smiling. Mother looked down the chute of the camera and took his picture.

The summer before, Grandmother had told me all about ESP. How by using Extra Sensory Perception, a person could have super human powers that could read people's minds or make then do things you wanted them to. So standing in the backyard, staring through a crack in the fence, I tried to use my mental power to hurry them up. I would die if any of my friends saw Father dressed in what I thought looked like a Halloween costume. But my parents took their sweet ole time, as if the picture had to be perfect for a fashion magazine.

Lately, Sheila had begun to revel in her position as Father's child of the year. Something she enjoyed without any competition from the rest of us. She marched right outside and, acting like Father's assistant, she stood next to him, holding his jacket while Mother took pictures of various stages of Father's dress.

That night, Sheila sat next to Father at the dinner table. When Father retired to the sofa to read, she slid up close to him with her own book in hand. For the past several months, she'd become his shadow, and he called her his "first mate." Wherever he went, she obediently followed.

Father's favoritism of Sheila caused a tug of war in my emotions. Never did I want to be his favorite, but at the same time I longed for him to notice me. Part of me wanted his approval, but only if it meant he never touched me. Unlike Sheila, just the thought of resting my body against his bony chest sent chills up my spine. And yet, I craved the same kind of relationship with him that he had with her. But Father acted like I didn't even exist.

Most of the time, Sheila seemed oblivious to the unfairness of Father's attention. She never bragged about her position, nor did I ever think she didn't love Mother or me. We were two kids in a play with different roles. One no better than the other. But when there were no roles to play, Sheila and I were the best of friends.

On the weekdays throughout the summer, Father came banging into our room before sunrise to wake Sheila up. In the dark, she fumbled around for her clothes while I pretended to be asleep. Only after the car doors slammed and the rattle of Father's VW bug faded down the street did I get out of bed.

On Saturdays, Father put on his kilt outfit and, with Sheila in tow, they left the house early in the evening, not to return until way after dark. Once, a large picture of Father decked out in his Scotch-Irish heritage, with Sheila standing proudly by his side, appeared across the front page of the Northern Virginia Sun. The picture, taken in a bar, made Father so proud. He carefully cut it out and taped it to the wall above his desk.

For days, he stood in the middle of the living room with his head high and arms crossed, staring at the picture. "Just look at my little first mate," he'd say, nodding his head up and down as if the rest of the world had finally caught up with the image he had of himself.

The purchase of the kilt set off Father's supreme arrogance. Convinced he could run our house like a Navy ship, he took over. If he didn't, he said, Mother would ruin us all.

"This house isn't big enough," Mother fought back. "There's no room for the kids to spread out. The bedrooms are too small and we need a basement. I shouldn't have to do laundry in the kitchen. There's just not enough room."

"Nobody needs more space than a sailor has on his ship," Father preached.

"Edmund," she said forcibly, "these are children, not sailors. Even with the bunk beds triple stacked, their rooms are too small. They can't even play a game on the limited floor space."

But Mother always lost the argument and made a hasty retreat upstairs to her room.

Determined to show Mother how it should be done, Father wasted no time getting everything shipshape. Beginning with the weekly menu, he chose spaghetti and meatballs for every Monday, Wednesday, and Friday night. He'd give us a special treat on Saturdays with Chinese carryout, but it would always be his favorite, Chop Suey. On Tuesdays he splurged on flank steaks, and on Thursdays, fish. For the life of me I can't remember what we had on Sundays.

Sheila and I tagged along on his first shopping trip as supreme ruler of the house. Leaning over the steering wheel of the VW bug he mumbled all the way to the strip mall on Columbia Pike. "If your mother would only listen to me, she wouldn't have so much work to do. Running a house is no different than running a ship."

The first spaghetti night, I sat down on the bench next to Mother, with Father sitting catty-corner to her. My brothers and sisters filled the remaining seats around the table. The fight between my parents that began a few days earlier had tightened to a quiet, tense silence. I never heard them yell. But when we kids sensed something coming, we knew to keep our mouths shut and stay out of their way.

Father broke the rigid silence by gloating, "Did any of you ever realize your Mother's meatballs looked like goat beans?"

Goat beans? Even to a kid, most of what Father said made no sense. I looked at my plate but Father's meatballs didn't look any different than the ones Mother made. Nobody answered, we just stared at our plates. Maybe, I hoped, ignoring Father would make him go away.

"What do you think, kids?" he went on. "Don't you think your Mother's meatballs look like goat beans?"

Without lifting my head, I rolled my eyes up and looked at Father. He glared at Mother while continuing to speak to us. Now he sounded like a bully on the playground. "You've seen goat beans, haven't you, kids?"

I looked at Mother, expecting any minute she'd start to cry, but she didn't. She sat there, slowly taking small bites of her spaghetti, without even glancing in Father's direction.

Now acting full of himself over his ability to accomplish what he felt she couldn't, Father rattled on, "Well kids, they're really small, like peanuts. That's how your Mother's meatballs look." His eyes stayed fixed on Mother. One side of his upper lip curled in a sneer. "See mine? See the size they are? That's how they're supposed to look."

I checked my meatballs again and they still didn't look any bigger than the ones Mother made.

Then the air shifted. Instinctively, I looked around the table to read each face. There were still no tears in Mother's eyes. She sat straight up on the bench and stared at Father. James's eyes shifted from person to person, taking note of everyone's position, most likely devising a plan to release some pressure out of the house. Nora and Brian sat obediently eating their spaghetti. Sheila kept a watchful eye on Father, probably looking for any chance to distract him away from Mother.

None of our schemes worked. While clearing the table, Mother said something to father, and things began to escalate. Father banged through the living room and sat down at his desk. When the clear bottle of vodka came out of the bottom drawer, I escaped upstairs to get lost in my latest book.

For about an hour, I managed to block out the world as I followed the adventures of Henry Huggins and his dog Ribsy. Just before sunset, I went downstairs to check the atmosphere of the house.

Standing on the bottom step, I took a deep breath before poking my head around the corner. To my left, James sat alone on the sofa, facing the dining room table. He held a thick book open in his hands, but I knew he was really reading Father.

Father had moved back to his seat in the dining room, his Luger now lying on the table in front of him. Mother sat opposite him with her elbows on the table and her chin rested firmly in the palms of her hands. Her long fingers wrapped tightly around the sides of her face, as if to steady her nerves. Father's never-ending barrage was now too slurred for me to understand.

I hated nights like this. They turned my chest into a big knot. The gun didn't scare me as much as I feared not being able to hold myself back. Everything in me wanted to run over and help Mother. But the knot paralyzed me, making me feel small.

My Mother's Song

It forced me to look to James, who at only twelve, acted more like an adult than anybody else.

Slowly, Father picked up the gun and turned it over, checking both sides. For several seconds, he stared at the Lugar, like he couldn't remember what he intended to do with it. He jerked his head a little to the side, as if his memory came back. In slow motion, he turned and pointed the gun between Mother's eyes.

Mother's spine stiffened and her hands came slowly down from her face. Father set his elbows on the table and wrapped both his hands around the gun. Squinting his eyes, his lips curled in. His jaw went out, and he started clicking his front teeth together in the most annoying way. "I can get you whenever I want," he slurred. "If you ever leave me, I will hunt you down and kill you."

Father lowered his head and I couldn't hear what he said. Then he and the gun leaned closer to Mother's face. "If I ever catch you with another goddamn man, I'll kill you both."

Mother didn't lean back or turn away. Without moving a muscle, she just kept staring at that gun.

James looked me in the eyes and motioned with his head for me to go back upstairs. Convinced he had a plan to take care of us, I skipped every other step on my way back up. I opened the door to our room and slipped inside, shutting it behind me. Sheila stood by the dresser, helping Nora put on her pajamas. I squatted down and in one big sweep, cleared a spot on the floor with my arm.

I had a good game of solitaire going when the yelling started. Sheila sat down next to me and leaned over and played a card from the pile. Quietly, we spoke without saying anything, just to hear our voices. The rows of cards were growing and the aces stacking up when I heard something being thrown.

Mother's heavy shoeless footsteps came charging up the stairs. The bathroom door slammed, and the water in the sink started running. I piled the cards up and smoothed the edges of the deck, then slid them back into their box.

Sheila helped Nora climb into her bed. I turned off the light and we sat in the dark with the hall light sneaking under the door. Then the red lights started pulsating through the window, their beams slapping against the walls.

I stayed frozen in our room wishing I could disappear. Closing my eyes, I pretended to believe in magic. With my mystical powers I created a new law. If any two people thought the exact same thing, at the exact same time, they would switch places. Quickly, I thought as many random thoughts as possible, hoping my magic would become real.

Unfamiliar footsteps came up the stairs. Feet carved shadows in the light underneath our door. Someone knocked on the bathroom door. The gentle voice of a policeman said, "Mrs. Gibson, it's safe to come out. Mr. Gibson is gone." I waited until their footsteps disappeared from the stairs before opening our door.

Sheila and Nora followed me into the hall. The red lights crept up the stairs. Around the sink in the bathroom were tissues covered with blood. In the dark Sheila timidly asked, "What do you think happened?"

"I don't know," I answered. "But the police are here, so we better get back in our room."

We waited in the dark about an hour before we heard more footsteps on the stairs. James opened the door and we tried to blink out the brightness of the hall light. Acting like a grown up, he stepped into the room. "Come on, girls. We have to go to the courthouse. Father's been arrested."

Nora and Brian were still in their pajamas when we climbed in the bus. James sat in the front seat with me right behind him. Mother's right hand shook as she reached for the gearshift. When I didn't see any blood on her face, I wondered if I imagined the dirty tissues in the bathroom.

The bus bumped as it entered the parking lot behind the courthouse. The tall brick structure wrapped around us on three sides. The weak floodlights high on the corners of the building did nothing to calm my fears. A chill ran up my spine at the thought of criminals behind those walls. What if Father is in there with a murderer? If he is, I thought, then he got what he deserved.

Mother stopped the car and turned around. "You guys sit still and obey James. I'll be right back." Her door popped open and she stepped out of the van. All alone, she walked across the parking lot and entered the building. My heart raced and I wanted to make the pounding stop. The confines of the van made the knot in my chest tighten like a noose around my heart. I wanted to open the door and run across the asphalt, do anything to release the tightness in my chest.

If I moved, even just tapped my foot, the racing settled down. If I sat still, I felt the knot thrashing, choking me and trying to pop through my chest. I feared any minute my body would explode.

The pressure became unbearable. I shook my feet. Then I got up and walked around inside the bus. I sat on the back seat then moved to the middle. I stood up and walked up and down the little aisle.

"James, make Ellen sit down," Brian yelled.

"All of you knock it off," he answered, still trying to act like a grownup.

I knew my movements bothered everybody, but I couldn't help it. I tried talking inside my head, desperately telling myself to sit still. But my chest kept throbbing. James turned around with his face red and his jaw clenched. A sure sign he was about to lose his temper. We all jumped when Mother, with a policeman by her side, opened the back hatch. I ran to the back seat to see what they doing. There, lined up on the ledge above the motor, were Father's rifles from the shed.

Mother's eyes were electric, they darted from the guns to the officer's face. She stretched out her hands with the palms facing up. Her voice quivered, "You don't understand; he has guns all over the house. He's going to kill me. My children aren't even safe. You have got to do something."

The officer calmly nodded while looking at Mother's now frantic face. His bland expression seemed to say Mother was some crazy woman over-reacting to her husband's harmless anger.

The knot in my chest ratcheted into high gear. Now I wanted to get up in the officer's face and yell, "Look here, buddy, my father's out of control! What's the matter with you? Can't you see how dangerous he is? He's so mean to my mother! I hate him and wish he would go away! Don't you get it?"

But somehow I knew it wouldn't do any good.

Mother kept talking about the guns, and the officer kept nodding. "I understand Mrs. Gibson, I understand." His disinterested expression never changed. The fact Father had all those guns didn't frighten him one bit. Finally, Mother gave up, lowered her arms, and dropped her head. Without looking at the officer, she slammed the hatch and walked back into the building.

My stomach churned. Looking around the bus at my siblings, I never felt so alone. Nobody cared about us, not even the police. The officer didn't care about Father's guns, the sight of them didn't scare him at all. He just didn't understand. If Father never came home, all our problems would go away.

When Mother climbed back behind the wheel of the bus, her fear had been replaced with a stiff-jawed defiance. Her head no longer hung down. She put her chin up and, with her eyes determined, we silently drove home in the dark.

For the next three days, Father stayed in what he called the "slammer." I spent those days in the quiet serenity of our home. Nobody yelled and nobody fought. It was like a big wind blew through the front door and pushed all our problems right out the back, leaving behind a big sigh of relief.

On the day we picked Father up from jail, he could barely contain his excitement. He sat in the front seat of the bus, talking to Mother about the slammer like it was nothing. I wanted him to shut up. Didn't he realize how embarrassed we were when the police came to our house? Had he forgotten he made Mother bleed?

My Mother's Song

We stopped for lunch at a deli and piled into a booth in the back. Alfred and James got to sit alone at a table behind us. Sheila and Brian sat next to Father on one side, and Nora and I sat with Mother on the other. Sheila leaned against Father and he put his arm around her shoulder. He kept rubbing Brian's hair saying, "I missed you, Mr. B." Not once did he speak to me, in fact, I have no memory of him even looking my way.

While we waited for our hamburgers and fries, Father spoke loudly, starting every sentence with, "In the slammer ..." Every time he used that word, Mother's face turned red. She leaned over and softly begged, "Edmund, please, we're in public. Everyone is staring."

But he kept right on talking. I don't know why Mother thought he cared if people stared at us.

That day at lunch, I realized something. For the first time, I considered the possibility that there might be more to the story of my parents' lives. More than what I saw. Maybe Mother had done something horrible that made Father act the way he did. Maybe there was another man. This new revelation gave me hope. If I knew what evil Mother did, then Father wouldn't seem so mean.

For weeks, I couldn't stop thinking about what Mother did to make father so mad. Every day I looked for an opportunity to ask Father about her. I didn't want to go on hating Father if Mother was guilty too. So I waited patiently for the perfect time to confront him.

One day, while I was sitting on a stepladder in the kitchen, waiting for a batch of oatmeal cookies to bake, Father came through the swinging door. In an unusually good mood, he was whistling the song with the chorus, "You take the high road and I'll take the low ..."

Seeing me there, he stopped and put his hands on the edge of the ladder. Leaning over me, he winked and said, "You're my prettiest girl, but don't tell your sisters."

His eyes were calm, with a bit of playfulness inside. My

moment had arrived. I stuttered something incoherent, trying to summon the courage to say the words I'd been rehearsing. Drawing in a deep breath I blurted it out, "Father, why are you so mean to Mother?"

Not exactly the words I intended to say, but they were out, and I breathed a sigh of relief.

In an instant his eyes clouded over and the playfulness died. Afraid of missing something, I sucked in a deep breath and didn't look away. His head pulled slightly back, his brows came together, and he bit his bottom lip. The expression froze on his face and he stared at me for what seemed like an hour. But I didn't budge, I just kept looking him in the eye, hoping for the explanation I'd been craving.

Without breaking our stare, his head turned slightly and he spit a piece of tobacco off the tip of his tongue. My fingers dug into my thighs in order to steady my nerves. I didn't regret asking the question. I really wanted to know the truth.

Father straightened up and, without saying a word, he turned and walked back through the swinging door. The door swung several times going *fwop, fwop, fwop,* faster and faster, until it stopped.

Although Father never said anything, I had my answer. Mother had done nothing to deserve his abuse. If she had, he would have told me. I gave him the opportunity, fair and square, to explain himself. But his silence meant he had no excuse.

From that day on, I felt justified in hating my father. Nothing he did would ever change my feelings. I decided he was mean just for the sake of being mean.

ALFRED

TO MY SURPRISE, THE SUMMER before I entered the fourth grade, Father let Sheila and me become Safety Patrols. Ever since the first grade, I'd envied those big kids with their silver badges and white belts as they stood at the street corner looking down on me from their position of authority. With their arms and legs spread-eagle, they seemed to dare me to challenge them. If only I had one of those belts, I'd be important too. I couldn't believe Father had said yes. Lately, it seemed, he always spoiled my fun. But not this time. Before the first day of school, he signed all the papers and proudly patted my shoulder as he handed them back to me.

At our first meeting, I begged and got the post on the median between the lanes where George Mason Drive crossed Columbus Street. Standing in the middle of the intersection seemed wildly dangerous. From there, I could see for at least a mile up and down both streets.

Every afternoon, I heard the shouts and laughter of the other kids long before they came down the hill on Columbus Street. When they crossed over George Mason Drive, their energy filled my domain as they gathered around me. In classic patrol position, I held them back from danger like they were wild ponies trying to cross Chiquatique.

One day, Sheila and I left school ten minutes early to get settled at our posts. Leaving her at the corner of Columbus and 14th Street, I headed down the hill to my post on the median. The crisp fall air sent a chill through my thin dress. I hated wearing the cardigan sweater Mother made me take to school, but I unwadded it and slid it on underneath my patrol belt. After buttoning it to my chin, I ran my fingers over the roughness of its little painted flowers.

Like a good soldier, I performed my duty and got all the kids home safely. Father's rigid rules forbade me to walk the short distance home alone, so I sat down on the curb and waited for Sheila to catch up with me. The cool concrete quickly penetrated my thin skirt so I bunched it up under my butt as much as I could. Why didn't I wear shorts under my dress? And what made Sheila always take so long? Everything seemed too quiet without the noise of the other kids and their banging lunch boxes.

Suddenly, off in the distance, police sirens wound up and grew closer and closer. Hoping to see the hook and ladder truck, I jumped to my feet. Within minutes, a huge fire engine, with lights blazing, went screaming by. A police car, its siren blasting followed right behind. With my eyes, I followed their flashing red lights until they abruptly stopped in front of the woods at the end of our street. Trouble, other than our family, rarely brewed on Buchanan Street, so I couldn't wait to find out what was going on.

Getting antsy, I paced the median, looking up the hill for Sheila. Finally, her mop of red hair appeared as she nonchalantly walked down the hill. "Come on, Sheila!" I yelled. "There's a fire! Hurry up!" Sheila was never nosy like me, so I verbally bullied her along. "Come on, come on, you're taking too long. RUN!"

From my post I saw the firemen pull the heavy hose across the grass into the woods. I didn't see any smoke, but there had to be a fire and I wanted to see the flames. When I looked back up the hill, Sheila had not made much progress. My words evidently failed to motivate her.

Clenching my jaw, I let out a growl. Maybe she didn't hear me. This time, I took a deep breath, cupped my hands around my mouth, and yelled at the top of my lungs, "Hurry up Sheila! Come on! There's a fire!" Still walking slowly, Sheila crossed onto the median, ignoring my now frantic pacing.

Finally, Sheila saw the fire truck and started to run. Together we sprinted down George Mason Drive to Buchanan Street.

Slapping our feet on the sidewalk, we both abruptly stopped at the curb across the street from the commotion. Other neighbors had begun to gather, and I still didn't see any smoke, but my nose confirmed the familiar smell of burning leaves.

At first, the police car parked on the other side of Buchanan Street looked empty. But when we walked by, we saw a young teenager sitting hunched over on the backseat. His head hung down and his arms were pulled back, obviously in handcuffs. He looked deep in thought, perhaps pondering his fate. Choking on her words, Sheila softly said, "Look Ellen, its Alfred."

My heart dropped from curiosity to dread. Yep, there'd be a fight at home tonight. Maybe not between Mother and Father, but definitely between Father and Alfred. The police will probably come to our house and all the neighbors will know Alfred started the fire. Everyone will be talking again about our family. I just couldn't understand why Alfred did things he knew would make Father mad. As if he needed a reason.

The excitement ended and the loud engine of the fire truck revved up and faded away. I didn't turn around to see the police car with Alfred drive off. Staring straight ahead, Sheila and I walked down Buchanan Street toward our house.

Halfway home I asked Sheila, "Do you think we should tell Mother?" Still staring straight ahead, she mumbled, "I don't know." And I knew she meant it. In spite of the cruel things my siblings and I did to each other, Sheila loved all of us the same. She had no favorites. She made it her mission to help all of us get along. So for her to decide whether or not to tell Mother about Alfred put her in a difficult situation. I knew it had to be my decision.

But I never knew what to do in a situation like this. Sheila wouldn't try to persuade me one way or the other. Timidly, she'd follow along with whatever I did. But at times like this I wished someone would tell me what to do.

"Maybe he's not in trouble," I said, trying to find hope. "Maybe the police were just talking to him because he knows who set the fire."

Taking our time, we climbed the few steps to our porch, and I pulled back the screen and walked through our open front door. Mother looked up from her seat on the sofa when we entered the living room. Without thinking, I blurted out all the words I'd mentally decided not to say. "Mother, there's a fire at the end of the street. It didn't look very big, and the firemen put it out. Alfred's in the police car. Do you think he started it? Do you think he's in trouble?"

As soon as the words left my mouth, I wished I hadn't said them. Mother's lips turned down and her face grew pale. "I don't know, Ellen," she said. Then she stood up, gathered up her needlepoint, and walked upstairs. Great, I thought, if I'd just kept my mouth shut, Mother would still be in the living room. Now I can't tell her about my day. All the stories built up inside me would have to wait. But for how long?

Since Alfred had become a teenager, Mother and Father didn't fight each other as much as they fought with, or about, Alfred. As the oldest, he was the first to challenge the rules. The first to explore life outside the walls of our house. I was six when he played us our first Beatles record. It seemed so defiant the way he hid it under his coat until he got upstairs. He shushed us all as we gathered around the blue record player. He turned the volume down real low. "Don't tell Father you heard this," he said, staring me dead in the eye.

I put my ear close to the speaker, drawn in by the beat.

"I want to hold your hand, I want to hold your haaaaand, I want to hold your hand."

Just one song convinced me Father would never like rock and roll. He and Mother both took music seriously. Mother taught us to read notes long before we started school. Our limited musical diet only included classical, marches, big bands, and a little jazz.

My Mother's Song

But Alfred did the thing Father dreaded most—he brought outside influences into our controlled household. He exposed us to the things Father thought were dangerous to our impressionable minds. He stirred in us the desire to know what else existed outside of Father's control.

It became a test of wills, with Alfred fighting for more and more freedom. When he grew his hair out, Father taunted him, calling him a "fag" and a "beatnik." But Alfred continued to goad Father. He skipped school and stayed out late. On April Fool's Day, he ignited Father's rage by filling the sugar bowl with salt. Father retaliated by making him eat the salt on his cereal every day until it was gone. Not one to give in, Alfred smiled and chewed each bite like it was drowned in syrup.

Then, in spite of both Mother and Father, he demanded we call him "Al," a nickname and a forbidden sin in our house.

After the name change, he began to separate himself from us. We became no more than suckers in his many attempts to take advantage of us younger kids. Once, after days of pestering to teach me how to play poker, he sat at the dining room table, shuffling a deck of cards. Chiding me, he said, "Come on, piglet, you want to learn how to play, don't you?" Then he banged the deck on its side and squeezed in the loose cards.

Mother yelled from across the room, "Alfred, don't call your sister names."

But he went on, "Come on, piglet, you can win money. You can double your allowance in one game. Come over here and I'll show you how."

Most of the time, Alfred ignored me much the way Father did. And like Father, I rarely wanted to spend time with Alfred. At the same time, I wanted him to want to spend time with me. His sharp wit and cutting comments hurt, yet I wanted to feel important to him anyway.

Realizing the ribbing was getting him nowhere, Alfred turned on the charm. "Come over here, Ellen, and sit down and I'll write out the hands. It's kind of like rummy, only you can win money." As I made my way to the table, a sweet tender smile broke out across his face. When I sat down, he leaned over and stared deep into my eyes. Once again, he sucked me right in.

Before I knew what happened, he'd written out the hands and slid the paper across the table. Before I even agreed, he had the cards dealt. He patiently kept explaining the rules like a caring teacher trying to help me understand a difficult problem.

Every time I lost a hand, he encouraged me to go on. "Oh, Ellen, give it another try, you're still learning. You lost because you're just a rookie. The more you play the better you'll get." By the time I figured out the hands, he had a chart made for my debt. When I protested, he offered me the biggest sucker play of all time, the "double or nothing." His charm faded when I finally called it quits. He didn't speak to me for the rest of the day.

On Saturday, when Father handed out our allowances, Alfred, with his palms up, stood right next to me. The minute my two quarters landed in my hand, Alfred demanded payment.

"Give it to me, Ellen, I won it fair and square!"

"No! It's my money," I yelled back, like the nine-year-old I was.

Alfred turned to father for support. "Ellen wanted to play poker and she lost. I told her how much she owed me, but she kept on playing. Her allowance belongs to me."

Father raised his eyebrows and looked down at me, "Did you play poker with him?"

"Yes, but …" I tried to answer, as tears pooled in my eyes.

Alfred kept pleading his case. "Come here, Father, I'll show you how much she owes me. I have a chart on the back of my door."

Father followed Alfred into his room, with me trailing right behind. Alfred shut the door and showed father the sheet of notebook paper he used to chart my debt. Underneath my name, he'd drawn thirteen little boxes, filled with the dates of the next thirteen Saturdays.

Father turned to me, "Well, Ellen, if you played and lost, you owe him the money." Then he walked away.

In tears, I threw my quarters at Alfred and stormed off to my room. Alfred yelled after me, "I don't know what you're blubbering about. You agreed to play." But my door slammed before he finished his sentence.

For three months I held my allowance for two seconds before Alfred snatched it away. For the next thirteen weeks, I gave him every penny and watched him smirk as he drew an "X" in each box. His smile now sickened me, because he had used it to take advantage of me.

As far as I knew, we Gibson kids got the biggest allowances on Buchanan Street. Unfortunately, as much as Father liked giving us the money, he hated taking us anywhere to spend it. Once the fence went up, only Alfred was allowed outside it. Occasionally, Mother took us to Bruce's Variety, but weeks could go by between trips. As the money built up in my pocket, I couldn't wait that long to spend it.

Not one to miss an opportunity to capitalize on our desperate situation, Alfred became our merchant. With his allowance, he walked to Bruce's and bought an assortment of cheap toys and candy he then sold to us at grossly inflated prices.

By the fall of '65, James too had earned his freedom from the back yard. One afternoon, he and Alfred walked to the new department store at Bailey's Crossroads. Relieved to be free of Alfred, I started a new jigsaw puzzle on the dining room table. Father sat in the folding chair at his desk. He had a book in his left hand, while the fingers on his right were wrapped around the bowl of his pipe. As he read, his lips sucked in, then blew out little puffs of white smoke.

Looking for straight edges, I spread out the puzzle pieces. When I heard the smack of Father's lips, I looked across the table as the red embers in the bowl of his pipe flared. When the glow died down, I went back to my puzzle until the next smack of his lips.

Just when Father's pipe and I had settled into an odd sort of rhythm, James came charging in, out of breath, through the front door. I caught a few key words as he tried explaining to father what had happened.

"We were at EJ Korvette's ... Alfred grabbed a bunch of records ... I ran ... the detective caught Alfred ..."

Mother came running down the stairs. Father jumped up from his chair.

"Where is he now?" Father demanded.

"I don't know, I just ran."

The intrusion frustrated me. So far, my evening had been peaceful. But leave it to Alfred to ignite Father yet again. To set him off like a match lit too close to an open gas burner.

Father paced back and forth across the living room. Agitated, he sucked spit through his front teeth, making a watery tisking sound. Mother stood in the dining room, watching him. Hoping to avoid the trouble, I slid my puzzle pieces off the edge of the table and into their box and quietly made my way through the living room and up the stairs.

I shut my bedroom door, muffling out Father's voice. Sheila set down her book and hung her head over the middle bunk. "What's going on?" she asked.

"Alfred's in trouble again. I think he stole something while James was with him at Korvetts. James took off and ran all the way home, but I think the police caught Alfred."

I cleared a spot on the floor and dumped my puzzle pieces out. Sheila jumped down off the bed, and we began poking through the pieces looking for straight edges.

Someone knocked on the front door and the voices quieted down. A stranger's voice now mixed with James and Father's. I recognized it as the familiar monotone of a policeman.

When all the voices stopped, I tiptoed down the stairs. The living room was empty and Father stood on the front porch smoking his pipe. "I've had it with this goddamn kid," he mumbled. "First the fire and now shoplifting. This time the state can just goddamn keep him."

That night, Alfred never came home. Somebody told me

Father gave him to "The State." I didn't know what that meant. I just hoped it never happened to me. I couldn't imagine living anywhere without my brothers and sisters.

After Alfred left, something inside me felt broken. Our family shifted, or tilted, off its axis. Up until then, I believed as long as all us kids stuck together, we would survive. The older kids looking out for the younger. All the way down the line. We were like a club, all united for the same cause. But not anymore. We'd lost an important member, and nobody seemed to care.

Father didn't join us when we visited Al at the Juvenile Detention Center a few days later. A nice policewoman led us into a small sterile room with long empty benches lined against the walls. A large window with little wires inside the glass looked into a big recreation room with a pool table, a sofa, and some chairs. Alfred stood leaning on a cue stick watching another boy playing pool. For some reason, he no longer seemed like my brother.

"Sit down and be still. I won't be long," Mother said as she followed the police lady into another room.

Sheila sat next to me, with Nora on her lap. James and Brian sat close to each other on the other side of the room. The smell of strong antiseptic made the place feel like a hospital. Even with all our eyes fixed on Alfred, he didn't look our way. I wanted to stand up and bang on the glass to get his attention. But I was afraid the police would stop me.

When Mother returned, the policewoman went into the rec room and pointed us out to Al. Acting surprised to see us, he set down his cue stick and walked toward the door. I don't know what I expected him to do, but it wasn't to just say, "Hi, guys," like we were all strangers on the playground. I wanted to tug on his sleeve, to make him look me in the eye, but he only paid attention to Mother. When he stood up and said "goodbye," I knew our family was forever changed. Alfred walked back over to the pool table and never turned around or waved goodbye. He picked up his cue stick and started to play like he'd never left.

But nobody told me he'd never come home again.

For the next several months, Father and Mother argued constantly. It didn't seem like Mother wanted to give Alfred away. She cried all the time, but not father. He seemed relieved to give Alfred to the State.

It bothered me the way Alfred no longer belonged with us. It all seemed unfinished. Like we took a kitten we no longer wanted and left it on the side of a country road. I couldn't stop thinking about him, and wishing somebody would give me more information.

Then one night, while helping Mother dry the dishes, I got the courage to ask her about Alfred. She was standing at the sink staring out the window with her hands buried deep in the soapy water. She pulled up a plate and, without looking down, started wiping it clean. Not one to endure long periods of silence, I chattered away about anything that came to my mind. Mother nodded but I don't think she heard me. She seemed more sad than usual.

Standing on the stepladder, with a towel in my hand, I picked up a plate and began to wipe it dry. Avoiding her eyes, I asked, "Mother, why did Alfred go away?"

Still staring out the window, she paused and thought for a moment. "He stole things from stores, Ellen. He broke into other peoples' houses. Then he refused to go to school."

"Do you still love him?"

Again, she kept her hands in the sink and thought for a moment. "Of course I love him." There was a catch in her voice, as if the pain swooped down upon her too quickly to stop it. "I love him because he's my son. But I don't like him much right now because of the things he's done."

The whole episode disturbed me because, like Alfred, I broke the rules too. I tried hard to obey my teachers, but I always got in trouble anyway. I seemed to constantly say the wrong things. How long, I wondered, before I became just like Alfred? How bad would Father let me be before he sent me away?

It took me a while to realize Alfred would never live with us again. When other kids asked where he went, I didn't know what to say. The only words that came out were, "He just doesn't live with us anymore." After all, how do you explain that your father gave your brother to "The State?"

In spite of how mean Alfred could be, I missed him. There were supposed to be six of us and Father made it five. Alfred did get away from Father, but he no longer had us. I don't think he ever realized how much he needed his brothers and sisters. He never seemed to understand the way we had to help each other out. To this day, I wonder if Alfred regretted getting sent away.

FATHER'S OTHER LIFE

MY FATHER LIVED TWO LIVES. For me, his least favorite child, I never saw the good one. But Sheila did. One Saturday night after she'd stayed out late with Father, Sheila came stumbling into our dark bedroom. I'd been waiting for her, laying there, wondering where she'd gone.

Earlier that day, Father pulled his heavy kilt out from the closet underneath the stairs. He laid it over the arm of the sofa where I sat reading a book. The scratchiness of the wool made my skin itch. It took him a long time to put each piece of the outfit on. I wondered if he picked the Buchanan plaid because we lived on Buchanan Street.

Sheila wore her favorite dress, the one with the lace V going down the front. I wasn't the least bit jealous, I had no desire to go anywhere with Father dressed like that. But Sheila loved it. She took his hand and they walked across the yard. Like Father was her knight in shining armor, he held open the passenger side of the bug, and she climbed in the front seat.

All day I'd been curious about where they went. Not that I worried about Sheila. I never thought Father would hurt her. But this time I wanted to make sure I wasn't missing anything fun.

Trying to be quiet, feeling her way across the room in the dark, Sheila changed into her nightie and climbed into bed. I waited for the creaking of the springs on the bunk bed below me before leaning over, "Where'd you go with father this time?"

Startled, she jumped. "Gee, Ellen, you scared the crap out of me. We only went to the VFW hall."

Poor thing. I'd been there before. One afternoon with all of us in tow, Father stopped there for a drink. He promised not to be very long, but he lied. We trailed him into the large wide-open room. The smell of too much cigarette smoke and not enough fresh air made my tongue taste like ashes. Tables were scattered over the open floor and small groups of men sat around them smoking and drinking. Father walked up to the bar, ordered a drink, and then shooed us away with a wave of his hand. He snatched the iceless drink off the bar and headed for a table.

Around those men, my father became a different person. With great ease, he sat around like he was a thoughtful professor talking about his favorite subject: black people. He smoked his pipe and listened patiently to the other men. Something he never did at home with us.

Just like at the gun shop, Father was the center of attention and other men moved closer to hear what he had to say. As he spoke, great swells of laughter filled the room. I never understood how anything my father said could be so funny.

"All this time, you've been at the VFW hall?"

"Yeah, Father got to talking and time flew by."

"How can you stand to go there? Doesn't the smoke burn your eyes?"

"No, I like it. I sit at the bar and Father lets me order all the Shirley Temples I want. Sometimes the guy behind the bar talks to me and gives me peanuts. I think it's fun."

I wouldn't mind going to the VFW and drinking Shirley Temples, but not with Father. Maybe if Mother went along, and I got to sit at a table with her and her friends. But Father's friends were different. I didn't know them. They weren't our neighbors or the parents of kids I knew. They weren't like Mrs. Haithcock, whose daughter Bonnie went to school with me.

In the summer of 1966, I finished the fourth grade and began to avoid going anywhere with Father. Not Sheila, as soon as school was out, she went to work with him everyday. I imagined hanging out at Father's office was miserable until the day she came home with a small paper sack full of all different colored hole punches. Sticking my hand in the bag, I grabbed a wad and let them fall through my fingers like confetti. "Where'd you get all these?" I asked.

"At work with Father," she said. "I go from desk to desk and everyone lets me have 'em. I've been collecting them for weeks."

For the first time, her trips with Father sounded like fun. "What else do you do there?"

"Well, there's a big field next to the buildings, and sometimes the Marine Corps Band practices out there. When they're there, I sit on the grass and listen to them play."

"Does father go with you?"

"No, I go by myself," she said, as if forgetting that, at home, we lived behind a six-foot fence. "There's also a Navy museum down by the river. Sometimes I go there."

"By yourself?"

"Uh huh," she said, taking back the bag. "Sometimes I go to the museum and just sit on the gun turrets."

"Aren't you afraid to be wandering all over by yourself?" I hoped her adventures were somewhat uncomfortable.

"No, there are soldiers everywhere. The whole place is fenced in with a guard at the gate. I'm never scared."

I couldn't believe it. Here, Father wouldn't let me out of the backyard, and yet Sheila could roam all over the Navy Yard by herself.

"Do you ever get anything to eat there?" I asked, dying to know what else I missed.

"There's a cafeteria next to the museum. At lunch time, we walk over there and Father lets me order whatever I want."

For a few minutes, I weighed the differences in Sheila's life and mine. I couldn't imagine Father ever taking me to work with him, much less any of the other places he went. Besides, I didn't want to go anyway. Especially since he never treated me as nice as he treated Sheila. And what would happen if I made him mad? What if he got as mad at me as he did Mother? No, I didn't want to take Sheila's place. For me, staying home in Mother's predictable world was better.

It would be years before I learned Sheila's adventures with Father were not always safe. Some nights, Father would be too drunk to drive them home. With his body slumped in the driver's seat, Sheila maneuvered around him and steered the car. One night, she told me, when Brian was five years old, he tagged along. Father got so drunk he couldn't drive. She and Brian got on either side of him and steered the car. At a snail's pace, they crept along for miles. Father's limp body shifted from one side of the driver's seat to the other. Fear tore Sheila to shreds. Not that she'd get hurt though; she only worried about getting Brian home safe.

Oddly, all the things about my father that caused me shame—his tattoos, his old age, his kilt and *lederhosen*—Sheila adored. She wasn't oblivious to the pain he caused—she knew he treated Mother badly. And she saw his unfairness toward the other kids. But we each had a role to play. I comforted Mother, and Sheila kept Father happy. In an odd sort of way, we knew it helped keep things under control. But, no matter what happened, Sheila and I never let those roles interfere with our friendship.

My father had two family lives. He and Sheila, and then the rest of us. In a way, Sheila kept him mollified with his fantasy family. She did a good job standing in for the rest of us.

Not once did I ever long to change places. And, in both worlds, and to this day, Sheila is still my big sister. And my very best friend. Nobody ever planned it that way, it just worked itself out and kept the family alive.

SEPARATION

IN JULY 1966, MY TENTH BIRTHDAY came and went without any notice from my father. A few weeks later, he drove home a present for himself.

To beat the August heat, Sheila and I were sitting at the dining room table cutting pictures out of magazines and gluing them onto construction paper. The motor of our new window air conditioner hummed just above our heads. Mother sat in her usual spot on the sofa in front of the big picture window. Like a metronome, she pushed and pulled a large threaded needle through the tightly pulled fabric of her latest needlepoint project.

I was blowing on the palm of my hand where I'd smeared a glob of Elmer's glue, when Father shoved open the front door and poked his head inside. "Come on mates, come see what I brought home."

Sheila jumped up and ran past Father as he held open the screen door. Mother set down her needle and thread and followed her. Not wanting to miss anything, I quickly peeled the new "skin" off my palm and bolted out the door. James came bounding down the stairs with Brian and Nora behind him.

There, parked at the curb, was a used-up black convertible 1962 Triumph TR3.

"What in heaven's name are we going to do with that?" Mother asked, raising her voice. "That's not a car for a family. The children need school clothes, we can barely afford to put food on the table, and you bring home a sports car?"

Father opened the passenger door and I poked my head inside. The nauseating smell of mildew and motor oil made the car seem old. Different sized gauges scattered along the dashboard like the cockpit of an airplane. To me, it looked like the miniature cars the clowns drove in the St. Patrick's Day Parade.

Sheila's long red hair bounced as she jumped up and down, begging Father to take her for a ride. Mother dropped her arms, balled her fists, and stormed back into the house. Father pushed the back of the front seat forward, "Climb in, mates."

Sheila climbed into the back where, instead of a seat, there was a ledge covered in carpet. Nora sat on her lap, while Brian and I squeezed in beside her. James plopped down on the front seat and stretched out his legs.

With a stiff grin, Father slid behind the wheel. Even though it was hot, he put on a pair of thin brown leather gloves with holes where his knuckles were. He revved the motor and jiggled the gearshift knob, and the car jerked forward. With a jolt, we took off up Buchanan Street.

With one hand on the steering wheel and the other resting on the shifter, father cruised George Mason Drive. Every time he punched the clutch to the floor, the engine whined in protest.

In the following days, Father and Mother fought constantly over the Triumph. Especially after Mother learned Mrs. Lane had loaned him the money. I don't recall the details because, by then, I'd become skilled at tuning them out.

By fall, the car began to rebel and sit dormant when Father turned the key. Many mornings, he came banging back inside swearing to "Jesus H. Christ," bellowing for us to get out of bed. With Father in the driver's seat, we lined up behind the rear bumper. With our hands on the trunk, we would push the car up Buchanan Street. When we'd gain enough speed, Father popped it in gear and the car bolted away from us. Without even waving goodbye, he'd give it gas and take off, leaving us halfway up the street.

Father's selfish purchase of the Triumph motivated Mother to invest in herself. Something inside her snapped, and she no longer seemed to care what Father thought. The day she joined a health club on the ground floor of the Calvert Apartments in

Alexandria, her expression changed. Her eyes brightened, her footsteps got lighter, and her chin lifted.

Unlike Father's sports car, the gym membership benefited the whole family. It included access to the indoor swimming pool on the top floor. So Mother enrolled us kids in swimming lessons. By the time school started, I could tread water for five minutes and swim the length of the pool.

At the gym, Mother let us take the elevator up to the pool by ourselves. With our towels over our shoulders, we piled in, sarcastically saying, "Thirteenth floor, please," knowing there was none. As the light skipped from the twelfth to the fourteenth floor, I'd snicker and say in my best cocky voice, "Suckerrrrs, you're really on the thirteenth floor and you don't know it."

As soon as the elevator opened, the smell of chlorine about knocked me off my feet. With the sunshine blinding us as it poured through the wall of sliding windows, we felt on top of the world.

On warm days, without screens or air conditioning, the windows were wide open. Sheila, Brian, and I couldn't resist spitting off the roof and watching the large wads of saliva change shape as they floated to the ground. Fearlessly, we leaned out and launched intricately folded paper airplanes. For what seemed like forever, the wind lifted them as they zigzagged across the treetops.

We were all happy at the gym. The pool gave Mother what Father never would, a break from us kids. With the handsome teenage lifeguards teaching us games like "Marco Polo," Mother never had to worry about us.

That same year, Mother got a new job as the production director for the quarterly magazine, *Music Educator's Journal.* The job fueled the passions she went to school for: music education, and publishing. Her desire for excellence fit well with the top-notch publication.

With her newfound confidence, Mother caved into her parents' request and asked Father for a divorce. When she wrote them with the news of the separation, my grandmother's reply was not surprising:

> *"One thing's for sure—we are most happy to see you happy after so many years of not being happy. You have such fine talents and so much basic training, it grieved us to see you robbed of all confidence in yourself ... do keep us informed on the progress of events—when will it all be finished?"*

Father complied. He packed some clothes and moved into a bright yellow house on Jackson Street near his favorite German bar, the *Bratwurst House*. The large Victorian home with a big wrap-around porch looked inviting. The first time I went there, I thought Father lived with a happy family.

With Alfred at the boys' home, and James now thirteen and busy with school, Sheila and I were left to look after Nora and Brian. So it was just the four of us the first time Mother dropped us off to visit Father.

In his ratty, dark-blue terrycloth robe, Father opened a side door and we stepped into a large kitchen. The morning sunlight bounced off the bright white cabinets. A small table sat in front of a bay window with yellow gingham curtains. "Wait here," he said. "I'll be right back." Then he left us to go get dressed.

Sheila and Nora backed into one corner, facing the table. Brian and I stood close to each other next to them. I expected any moment for a woman to appear to fix breakfast. But none showed up.

After a few minutes, an older man we'd never met came in and poured a bowl of cereal. Setting a bottle of milk on the table, he sat down and stared at us. "So you're Ed's kids, huh? What are your names?"

I looked around for his wife but, still, no woman appeared. Nervously, I told him my name and introduced my siblings.

Then I tried to use ESP to make him leave. But, as usual, it didn't work.

Finally, Father returned, dressed in a blue shirt and white shorts. "Come on mates, let's go." He whistled as we crossed the yard to the Triumph. Sheila climbed into the front seat and Brian and I quickly scooted in the back next to the windows, leaving Nora the least favorite spot in the middle.

Once we got going, I slid onto the edge of the bench and stuck my face between Father's head and his open window. The hot summer air disappeared when Father pulled onto the main road. Letting my hair blow straight back, I imagined we were riding with the top down.

As we cruised along the George Washington Parkway, I didn't care if he ever stopped. With the hills and woods on one side, and the Potomac River weaving along on the other, the view from every window was spectacular. Every now and then, when the road came close to the river, I could smell the musty odor of the polluted water.

After a few minutes, Father pulled off the road into the gravel parking lot of a large marina. Though beautiful from a distance, the closer you got to the river, the uglier it became. Before we slammed the car doors, I smelled the putrid trash that floated on top. I breathed through my mouth as we walked toward the rows of white boats tied up along the narrow docks. On top of the water, brownish foam bobbed up and down, leaving a grimy film along the bottom of the boats.

"I've been here before," Sheila said.

Curling my lip and wrinkling my nose, I sneered at her.

"I have," she said. "Father and I go sailing here sometimes. He rents one of those boats and we go out on the river. I have to be careful because if I don't duck when he says to I can be knocked into the water."

The thought of an adventure lifted my spirits. Maybe that was why Father brought us here, maybe he planned to take us all sailing. But Father didn't say a word about it as we walked up and down the docks looking at the boats.

"We go in a boat like that," Sheila said, pointing to a small boat on the water with its sail protesting against a strong wind. "Father sits at one end, and I sit in front of him. See how the guy is holding onto the rope attached to the sail? That's what Father does. That thing on the back—it's called a rudder—it's what he uses to steer. When he wants to turn, he shouts "duck," and I crouch down while the bottom of the sail moves to the other side."

I looked out on the river and imagined Sheila and Father in the boat, their eyes squinting in the sun. I imagined Father at the back, his hand on the rudder, the sail filled with wind. I imagined them laughing, having the time of their lives.

Fury welled up inside me. Why couldn't Father be fair? Why did he leave the rest of us trapped in the backyard while he and Sheila took off on their grand adventures? How could he constantly go out and spend money having fun with Sheila, knowing we were home broke?

Brian ran up the dock next to Father, his footsteps echoing off the hollow space between the wood and the water. Father held tight to Nora's hand. My steps got smaller and smaller as I fell further behind. Brian chattered to father while pointing to the boats and the sails. Father picked up Nora and carried her on his shoulders.

But that day at the marina, nothing Father did could convince me he cared one bit about me. All I wanted him to do was to hurry up and take me home.

Back in the car, Father's good mood hadn't dimmed. "Let's go get some chow. What do you think of that Mr. B? My first mate and I know just the place."

When Father turned off Columbia Pike, the car jolted into the parking lot of his favorite Italian restaurant. The car crept up the steep hill into a parking space in front of the white stucco building. The tangy tomato smell of spaghetti greeted us ten feet from the door.

Inside, Sheila knew exactly where to sit. She slid into one side of a booth, and I climbed in opposite her. Father and Brian filled the rest of her bench and Nora shimmied up next to me. When the waiter came over, Father grinned like the most adoring of fathers, "Humm," he said rubbing the whiskers on his chin. Then he waved his arm toward us in one big sweeping gesture. "Let them have whatever they want."

We all ordered our food with large cokes and the waiter walked away. With a twinkle in his eyes, Father leaned over and began reciting his favorite story, *The Tell-Tale Heart*. His smooth deep voice rattled out the words.

"True! —nervous—very nervous I had been and am: but why will you say that I am mad?"

As much as I hated the story, it was impossible to tune him out. Father made it all seem so real. His deep actor's voice carefully pronounced each word for the most powerful impact. He leaned in close to each of us, going from me to Brian, then to Sheila. He even looked at Nora, who, at five, I doubted understood the horror of the story. Brian became mesmerized, unable to look away. With our mouths hanging open, we followed every move Father made. He knew the perfect places to pause and build the suspense.

In order to distract myself from my mental image of the "eye," I tried to focus on the clinking of the dishes from the kitchen. I tried to eavesdrop on the loud family behind us. But it didn't do any good. Father's riveting voice sucked me in and I found myself hanging on his every word.

"… I made up my mind to take the life of the old man, and thus rid myself of the eye forever."

Like a metal brush, the hair on the back of my neck rose up and poked me. My scalp shrank. I tucked my hands under my thighs, preparing for the scariest part. Father hunched over and spoke slower and softer like he was telling a secret.

"… I threw open the lantern and leaped into the room. He shrieked once—once only. In an instant I dragged him to the floor and pulled the heavy bed over him. I then smiled gaily …"

Before Father could finish the sentence, a man with a gun jumped in front of our table. My eyes flared open at the sight of the little black metal barrel. I stared as he aimed it at Sheila. My heart shot into my throat and kept me from screaming. I kept telling myself, it's not real, yes it is, nah, it can't be.

With a big smile, the man turned, pointed the gun at me, and pulled the trigger. The hammer came down with a flat click, like one of Brian's empty cap guns. Relieved, I let out a deep breath. It wasn't real. Then he turned the gun to Sheila and it clicked again. Then Brian, and a click. He even turned it to Nora and pulled the trigger.

As soon as the gun made its final click, Father slapped the table, threw back his head, and broke out in gut-wrenching laughter. The man with the toy gun doubled over and held his stomach, laughing hysterically. Brian's mouth gaped wide open. Nora looked around as if she'd missed the joke. Sheila's eyes widened in confused fear. As Father and the man laughed, I tried to figure out if what I saw really did happen.

The gunman disappeared as quickly as he appeared. When Father didn't go after him, I knew he'd set it all up. All through our dinner, he kept bursting out laughing. Awkwardly, we laughed with him without understanding why.

Back at our house, Father sat in the car until we were all inside. Last to go in, I used my whole body as leverage to slam the door shut. The whine of the Triumph revved up as Father gunned the engine. As the sound disappeared down the road, I hoped he never came back.

I never told Mother about the man and the toy gun. And I don't think anyone else did either. The whole thing seemed too unreal. Too unbelievable to explain.

When I crawled in bed that night, I still hoped Father would never come home. Life with him had become too unpredictable. Too difficult to tell the difference between the real and fake violence. Even the horror stories he told now seemed real. Without him around, I didn't have to try and figure it all out.

Several weeks went by, and Father didn't return to the house. But late one evening, after swimming, we saw him at the gym. Sheila and I were sitting opposite each other on the big sofas in the lobby. Nora and Brian were on the floor playing with Matchbox cars. Mother was still in the back, finishing up her workout.

The door flung open and hit a little bell, announcing my father's arrival back into my life. He'd shaved off his beard and at first I didn't recognize him. He almost looked respectable, like the other kids' dads. But I didn't trust this new man. Something about the change in him unsettled me.

He sat down next to Sheila, leaned over close to her face, and whispered something in her ear. Sheila turned toward him and shook her head *no*. Looking dissatisfied, Father got up and walked over to me. He sat down sideways beside me on the sofa. I could tell he'd just taken a bath, because he smelled like fresh soap. The patch of gray hair behind his receding hairline was combed neatly forward in short narrow bangs across his forehead. His black slacks were neatly pressed and he was wearing his burgundy blazer with the University of Manchester patch on the breast pocket. The collar of his dingy white shirt was bunched up underneath his tightly tied bow tie.

"What's your mother been doing?" he said, trying to act like he cared.

I shrugged and wanted to say "nothing." But I knew better. With Father, part of me always feared saying the wrong thing and part of me feared saying nothing at all.

"I don't know ... working ... taking us to school," I managed to stammer out.

"Have any men come to the house while I've been gone?"

What a stupid question. Mother never talked to any men, much less had one come to the house. Something about the look in his eyes annoyed me. His eyeballs slightly twitched from side to side. Once again I was afraid to answer and afraid not to.

I looked deep into his eyes for signs of a motive. They weren't angry or watery like when he had too much to drink. But I still didn't trust him. Was he being nice in order to trick me into saying something to hurt Mother? Feeling trapped, I bit the inside of my lip as the air between us grew stale.

Thinking I better answer, I sucked in a gulp and uttered a plain, "No." Then I tapped my foot to distract myself from looking at his face. I squinted my eyes to focus hard on making him leave, hoping my ESP would move him out the door. If Mother saw him, they might get in a fight right there in public.

At my answer, Father's eyes went flat. The smirk on his face disappeared and he stood up. Without saying goodbye, he walked out the door, and the little bell announced his departure. I followed his profile as he walked past the window and got into his car.

A few minutes later, Mother came out with her cheeks beaming red from exercise. She looked so happy, nobody dared ruin it by telling her that we'd had company.

But Mother's fear began to take over our lives. At the A&P, she scouted out the parking lot for Father's car before letting us go inside. At the library, her fear forced her to circle the building several times, before giving us an "all clear" to enter. It even kept us away from the gym, the one place we all enjoyed.

Then one day the separation ended. We came home from school and Father's car was parked in the driveway. My heart sank when I saw him lying on one of the benches in the dining room, with his head in Mother's lap. When he saw us, he jumped up, and with a grand bow he said, "Hello, children, your adoring father is home."

Dramatically, he put his arms around Mother and did something I'd never seen before, nor would I ever see again—he kissed her on the lips.

Like a giddy teenager in love, he looked Mother in the eyes

and released a swarm of endearing compliments. "Josephine, you are the most beautiful woman that ever lived. The smartest and most talented woman in the world."

At first I fell for the entire performance. Wanting him so badly to be the man I was seeing, I took it all in. For so long I'd dreamed of being part of a normal family that I jumped at the first weak sign of it coming true. Even though, in my gut, I could tell Mother just played along. Her eyes didn't show any passion and, when she smiled, they didn't sparkle.

But everything in me wanted to believe my father had become a different man. I'd spent too many years dreaming of what it must be like when your parents are in love. I wanted it so badly, I bought the whole show.

My grandmother wasn't so fooled. In a four-page barrage against Father first, then Mother for taking him back, she wrote:

> ... *He has forced you to live in poverty of slum proportions for all these years. He has abused you in public and private in such a way as to make angels weep.*
>
> *In fact ... he has forfeited for all time any and all consideration from us. This happened when Ellen was born.*
>
> *But so long as he can sweet talk you into standing still while he beats you—he is yours—and we say not a word about your decision. You might (underscored four times) be able to return to civilized life with him in the house, but I couldn't ...*

After Father's return, visits and letters from my grandparents stopped. Mother didn't even talk about them any more. At Christmas, no big box arrived tied up with grandfather's string. Only one small card came, without any money inside for presents. And Mother never told us why they disappeared.

It didn't take long for life in the Gibson house to go back to the frightening world we knew best. The bottle of vodka returned to the deep desk drawer. Father slept on the pullout sofa with his loaded Luger on the end table. Once again, he began to bully Mother.

In December of that year, his mental cruelty hit a new low. It all began when he decided we all, even Mother, needed music lessons. One night a week, with the Gilbert and Sullivan songbook on the music stand, he made us line up.

Standing erect in front of us, Father demonstrated how to draw in a deep breath. He put his hand on his stomach, made a little slit with his lips, and sucked in some air. He modeled the best posture to squeeze in our stomach muscles. And coached us to push the air from deep within our diaphragms.

I stood tall and tried hard to concentrate while I sang out the words, "I am the Captain of the Pinafore! And a right good captain, too!"

Father pranced around us like a big show-off. His deep baritone voice drowning us out. Every so often, without stopping his singing, he placed his hand in front of our mouths, checking for that sneaky escaping air. If he felt it, he bellowed, "Tighten up those muscles, mate! Sing out!"

The singing wasn't such a bad exercise. That is, until December 20th, the night of Mother's birthday. That night, Father arranged us in two semi-circles in the living room. In front Nora, Mother, and me sat in folding chairs. Behind us stood James, Brian, and Sheila.

After unfolding the silver music stand, he set the *Army Navy Hymnal* on the ledge. He licked his finger and rustled through the pages until he found his favorite Christmas carol, "God Rest Ye Merry Gentlemen."

Mother didn't look happy when we started to sing. Father, our conductor, stood in front of us, with his shoulders back, waving his baton in large sweeping circles. He swayed from side to side, sporadically lifting his left hand, our sign to hold a note. Squeezing in my stomach muscles, I felt for that escaping air as I sang.

"God rest ye merry gentlemen, Let nothing you dismay."

We had just finished the first line when someone knocked on the front door. Father walked over and opened it to our next-door neighbor, Mrs. Rouse.

In her soft southern drawl she said, "Edmund, all Jo's friends are next door for her party. Can you send her over?"

How nice, I thought. Mother's friends are having a party for her birthday.

But then I couldn't believe what Father said. "I'm sorry, it's a family night and we're singing Christmas carols." Then he shut the door in Mrs. Rouse's face.

Trying to hide my shock, my eyes darted to Mother. Her face grew stiff. Her eyes filled with tears, but she held them back. Father picked up his baton and said, "Let's start at the second verse."

Once again we all joined in, "From God our heavenly Father a blessed angel came."

We didn't finish the verse before there was another knock. Father told us to keep singing. He got up and opened the door to Mother's friend, Mrs. Haithcock. "Edmund, all Jo's friends are next door, won't you let her come to her party?"

I mouthed the words without singing in order to hear Father's response. Without any emotion, as if discussing the weather, he said, "I'm sorry, she can't come over tonight. It's a family night and she's singing Christmas carols with her children."

Mrs. Haithcock's head went down. Mother could no longer hold back her tears. She blinked and huge puddles of tears squeezed out her eyes. Father came back to the "choir" and resumed conducting.

I tried to sing, ignoring the nausea churning in my stomach. My jaw clenched in hatred toward my father. My heart broke in two at the sight of Mother's tears.

During the third verse, there was another knock on the door. Father again ordered us to keep singing. He calmly walked over and opened the door. I couldn't see who it was or hear the conversation. I looked at Mother and she kept on singing while tears continued to puddle inside her lower eyelids. When she blinked, they dropped out, rolled down her chubby cheeks, and fell like little raindrops off her chin. But she kept right on singing.

Feeling helpless, I tried to ignore what had just happened. Father shut the door and walked around us. He waved his baton in the air with a gleam in his eyes. Mother sat there all evening, singing and crying at the same time. I couldn't look at her and hold back my own tears.

From our living room, I heard the partygoers saying goodbye. I heard their car doors slam and their engines start. I heard them drive away.

In bed that night, I pulled my covers over my face and cried. My tears turned to rage for my inability to save my mother from my father. If only I'd known about the party, I could have distracted him. If only Mother had gotten that divorce.

I never understood how Father bore the sight of the sadness he caused. How he lived with himself after sending those nice ladies away. Why didn't he want Mother to have a good life? Did he come home just to cause her more pain?

In my opinion, Father never cared about anyone but himself. He didn't even like Mother and yet, when he had the chance to go away, he begged to come back. To him, we were nothing more than possessions, no different than his Triumph. But when we no longer met his expectations, he cursed us then recklessly cast us aside.

TWO VIEWS

FATHER'S ARREST IN THE SUMMER of '65 increased the ever-growing canyon between him and Mother. The wall of silence grew as tall as the fence "shielding" us from our neighbors. Most days, Father came home, cooked dinner, then he and Sheila left.

As usual, long after dark, Sheila came stumbling into our room. From the top bunk, I could smell the stale tobacco that lingered on her clothes. For most of our lives, Sheila and I had been inseparable. Only our father took us apart.

Always a good student, James spent more and more time on his schoolwork. Many Saturday afternoons, Mother dropped him off at the library and didn't pick him up until closing time. When he was home, he sat for hours hunched over his books at the small desk in the boys' room.

One night, after Mother left Brian and Nora at home with James, I sat alone on the backseat of the bus as she pulled to the stoplight at the intersection of Columbus Street and Columbia Pike. The red light lit the tears glistening on her face. The sounds of the fight back at the house had been muffled behind the closed bedroom door, I hadn't heard a word. But I did sense it was happening again.

The bus's engine rattled the way only a VW does. The cars on Columbia Pike whizzed by while we waited. Mother's silent tears made me feel helpless. My chest throbbed as if something heavy pressed against my heart. Anger toward Father for making her cry boiled to the surface. I wanted to do something, somehow fight back, but I felt too small. Sitting there alone I thought, when I get older, I'll find a way to make her life better. I'll get rich and buy her a mansion and hire maids to clean it.

The light turned green and the engine whirled as Mother

pulled into the intersection. Somewhere off Columbia Pike, we turned down a road with no streetlights. On the right, spooky woods crept up to the curb. The other side was lined with small houses with sloping flat roofs. The front yards banked up from the road, then leveled off at the houses, then banked up sharp in the back. Most of the homes were dark, without so much as a porch light on. It reminded me of the scary streets in the big Alfred Hitchcock book Father sometimes read to us.

I'd never heard of a psychiatrist before, and I wasn't sure what he did for Mother, but we came here regularly. Mother called him a doctor and called this his "office." But it looked more like a house to me.

Mother drove past the office, made a U-turn, and parked the bus in front of the sidewalk leading to the front door. When she turned off the headlights and the engine stopped, it took my eyes a second to adjust to the dark. Mother looked in the rearview mirror and wiped her tears off with the palm of her hand. I crawled across the seat, grateful the door opened onto the sidewalk and not into the woods. When I jumped out and slammed the door, I heard the far-off sound of the cars on Columbia Pike. A breeze rustled the trees and somewhere, off in the distance, a creek gurgled, probably Four Mile Run.

Mother breathed hard as she lifted her heavy body up the concrete steps. She opened the front door and we stepped into the waiting room that looked more like a living room. As usual, the office didn't have any kid's stuff. No *Highlights* magazines or coloring books and crayons. Preparing for at least an hour of boredom, I shimmied up onto a stiff leather sofa and put my elbow on the silver metal armrest. My feet stuck straight out.

Hoping to find something interesting, I glanced around the room at the dark wood paneling and cheap paintings of rivers and mountains and other places I had never been. Mother disappeared behind a wood door stained the same color as the walls.

When Father walked in, the skin on the back of my neck

drew tight and tugged at my scalp. Without saying a word, he looked straight at me and then headed toward the room Mother had entered.

It was all wrong. I recognized the arrogant expression on his face. It was the same look he gave Mother when he criticized her. I knew he shouldn't be here. Sensing something embarrassing was about to happen, I wanted to run, but felt stuck to my chair.

Father shoved open the door, giving me a clear view of the psychiatrist sitting behind a dark brown desk. A mop of thick grey hair covered his head almost to his eyebrows. His salt-and-pepper untrimmed beard covered most of his face. Casually, Father walked around the desk, reached into his jacket, and pulled out his Luger. He pulled back on the slide of the gun and it clicked, then he put the tip of the barrel up against the hairy man's head.

From my viewpoint, I couldn't see or hear Mother, but I knew she was there too.

The doctor stiffened and did not move. His eyes flared open and he stared straight through the door at me, but really he looked right through me. Father nonchalantly leaned over and whispered something in his ear. The man still didn't move.

Two things kept running through my mind. The first thought was, this isn't real. I'm making it up. Father does not have a gun pointed at this man. Then I debated with myself. No, this is real. I am watching Father hold a gun to a man's head. My mother is sitting there watching it happen. Hoping to get Father to disappear, I sat perfectly still and mentally tried to get him to leave the office.

Father looking relaxed, sat down on the edge of the desk. While still holding the gun against the man's head, he rested his elbow on his thigh and crossed his right leg over his left. Except for the gun and the man's big eyes, you'd think Father was chatting up an old friend.

While Father talked, the psychiatrist never turned his head.

Even his eyes didn't cut in Father's direction. It was like Father was Jack Frost and he said "freeze" and the man turned into a solid piece of ice.

Finally, Father stood up and eased the slide of his gun back into place. He turned around, left the office and walked into the waiting room. I tried to look him in the eye, but he didn't even see me. With that annoying smirk on his face, he put the Luger in the holster under his arm and slammed the front door on his way out.

As soon as I turned my head, Mother, in a panic, came walking toward me. She made a quick scan of the room, looking for Father. Her hands shook as she reached for the doorknob. She poked her head out the front door before stepping onto the porch.

Afraid she'd forget me, I jumped off the sofa and ran after her. Mother had the car in gear before I slammed the back door. She gunned the engine and drove like a mad woman down the narrow dark road. I wanted to ask her what Father was doing, and why he had the gun, but I was still wondering if I had imagined it all.

The bus jolted up the driveway in front of our house. Mother was out the door and on the porch before I caught up with her. When we walked into the house, James must have sensed trouble, because he jumped off the sofa the minute he saw us. Nora and Brian, who were playing cards on the living room floor, immediately stopped and stood up too.

Mother slammed the front door behind us and rattled off orders like a drill sergeant. "James, get the younger kids' pajamas. Ellen, get yours. And hurry up, we need to leave as quick as possible." James didn't ask any questions and Mother didn't say anything about Father.

When we piled into the bus, I didn't have the energy to fight for the window seat. Mother and James ran back in the house and came out carrying the large wooden box with James' coin collection, "just in case we need some money," Mother said. I wasn't afraid, but the knot inside me pressed against my chest. I stuck my feet straight out on the seat and moved them back and forth like windshield wipers, hoping to settle down.

Mother drove frantically down Buchanan Street. The engine sounded tired as she banged each gear into place. Half way to Columbia Pike, she made a sharp turn into the apartment complex on the other side of the cul-de-sac at the end of our street. She turned off the headlights and the bus crept along in the dark. Then she leaned over and killed the engine. The scratchy sound of the tires went slower and slower as we coasted into a space between two trees. A position that gave us a clear view of our house. In silence we sat there for what seemed like hours.

A million questions spun around in my head. If I thought about them, the knot in my chest tightened. Something did happen at the psychiatrist's office, but did I imagine the gun? And where in the world was Sheila? Did anybody know? What would happen after tonight? Would we ever go home again? Each question created another question, so I tried to think about something else.

Just when my knot started to wind down, Mother sat up straight and leaned over the steering wheel. "There he is," she whispered. Poking my head over the console between Mother and James, I stared down our dark street. Father's silhouette, with Sheila following close behind, skipped up the steps and disappeared onto our porch.

Mother let out a big sigh and started the engine. She didn't turn on the headlights until we got to Columbus Street.

There weren't many cars on the road as we drove across town. We waited in the car while she got a room at the Highlander Hotel. I changed into my nightgown and lay next to Mother on one of the beds. The big lights from the parking lot peeked through the blinds, making stripes on the ceiling. Every so often, headlights glared through the blinds and crept across the walls.

I still wasn't afraid, but my pulse pounded in my throat. I looked down at my chest, certain I could see my heart beating.

I tried breathing real deep, holding it in until I had to breathe again. But my heart thumped so hard it kept me awake.

Sensing my problem, Mother leaned over and whispered, "See the holes on the ceiling?"

The crooked tiles did have tons of tiny holes spattered all over them.

"When I can't sleep, I count the holes."

Trying to lay still, I stared at the tiles and started counting. Every few minutes another car went by. The headlights, split apart by the blinds, swept across my holes like little floodlights announcing the arrival of a starlet. In the distraction, I lost count and forgot where I started. Somewhere in the sea of holes, I fell asleep.

The next morning, I woke to the sun pouring through the blinds. In another room, a toilet flushed and the water rushed through a pipe in the wall. I didn't want to get up. The dots on the ceiling brought back the memory of the night before. Couldn't we just stay in the hotel room all day? We'd be safe here because Father didn't know where we were.

Mother rolled over and shook me. "Get up, Ellen, and get dressed. I need you to help Nora and Brian." I put on my clothes from the day before and sat on the edge of the bed. James was already up and helping Brian with his clothes.

Mother dropped James off at his school before driving Brian and me to Claremont. She never said a word about what happened. When I entered our classroom, Sheila was already in her seat. Something about the night before made my family feel different. It didn't seem right. Sheila and I always walked to school together. It reminded me of the day Alfred went away.

I didn't even think to ask her where she had been all night.

But many years later, I told her about Father and the psychiatrist. She laughed and said, "Ellen, I was there too."

"No you weren't, Sheila. I distinctly remember being by myself in the waiting room."

"No, Ellen," she said. "That night, I rode there with Father.

When he went inside the house, I ran up onto the porch and looked through the window. I saw the whole thing."

"Did you see me?" I asked.

"No," she answered. "I thought I was alone."

"Huh, me too."

CHRISTMAS

IT RARELY SNOWS IN DC ON CHRISTMAS DAY, but in 1966 we had seven inches. On Saturday, Christmas Eve, I jumped down from the top bunk and used my fist to wipe a small peephole in the thin layer of frost on our cold bedroom window. The clean white snow blanketed our entire neighborhood, blending it all together, making our house appear as serene as everyone else's.

Shivering in my thin nightgown, I ran downstairs and plopped on the floor in front of the big vent that warmed our living room. Drawing in a deep breath of the dry air, I smelled the slight scent of gas from the furnace. Tucking my knees tight to my chest, I stretched my nightgown over them and rocked back and forth. It wasn't long before the banging of my siblings upstairs invaded my peace. Shucks, now I'd have to share my spot with one of them.

The pullout sofa in the living room where Father slept was folded up and he was gone. No fights had erupted the night before, and so far this morning, Mother remained peacefully behind her bedroom door. No tension filled the house, so the day held promise.

All week, I'd noticed every other house on Buchanan Street had their Christmas trees. The lights taunted me from their picture windows. Their presence reminding me how we Gibson's were always the last family to start Christmas. Father never put our tree up before Christmas Eve, and now with the snow, I wondered if he would bother. Sheila was the next one downstairs, so I slid over and we sat back to back, trying to keep warm.

At ten and eleven years old, we were almost too big to both fit in front of the vent. But winter mornings wouldn't be the same without our ritual. Silently, we both stared out the window at the falling snow. When Brian came downstairs, I stood up to give him a turn to get warm and I headed to the kitchen for a bowl of cereal.

While I watched milk splash over my Sugar Pops, the backdoor opened, and Father stood in the doorway, stomping snow off his boots. Snowflakes floated down off the black beret tilted sideways on his head. Clumps of his beard were frozen together like little icicles. He let out a deep sigh and rubbed his gloved hands together.

Meticulously brushing snow off his coat, father didn't seem to notice me sitting at the table. Cautiously, I stared at him for any sign of aggravation, hoping the snow wouldn't make him mad. Bracing for the worst, I held my breath and prepared for the peace to blow out as he stepped in, but it didn't. And since he wasn't swearing or cursing the weather, the day still held promise. Without saying a word to me, he walked through the swinging door into the living room.

Before the door swung back, I stopped it with my foot and stood in the doorway. James was up and now stretched out on the sofa. Brian and Sheila sat cross-legged in front of the vent.

"Come on, James," Father said. "Get dressed. We're going to build a sled. We're all going to get the tree."

Ah ha! There would be a Christmas, and Father even seemed excited.

James headed upstairs and I stepped aside as father walked through the kitchen and out the back door. Despite the snow, he and James worked all morning in the backyard building a sled. After lunch, they pulled it around to the front of the house. The sled was the ugliest thing I ever saw. The two-by-fours runners were so thick I wondered how they'd ever slide over the snow. The plywood on top had small pieces of wood sticking up; built-in splinters just waiting for our little butts.

Eagerly, Mother stood inside the closet underneath the stairs, handing out our coats. She wrapped a long scarf three times around my neck, as I spit out the little bits of mohair that flew in my mouth. She bent over and held the top of my plastic boots while I pushed hard to get them over my shoes and two pairs of thick socks. We lined up as she helped us stuff our pant legs deep inside our boots. She shoved my mittens on until my fingers were all the way to the ends. When she finished, we all looked the same, only different heights.

The snow had stopped falling when James and Father picked up the thick rope and started pulling the sled across the yard. Sheila, Father's faithful companion, walked next to him. Nora and Brian struggled to keep up. I lagged behind, keeping step to the crunch of their boots on the fresh snow.

About halfway up Buchanan Street, Nora and Brian started to get tired. Father stopped the sled and gently picked them up and set them on top. The grey sky hovered thick around us, without a blink of sunlight getting through, a sure sign of more snow to come. Slowly, we made our way down the median of George Mason Drive.

When we stopped at the intersection of Columbia Pike, I jumped with excitement at the sight of the tree stand in the parking lot of the shopping center across the street. When the light changed, Father and James got a boost of energy, and we ran across the street. I just couldn't wait to get our tree and start Christmas.

Leaving our clunky sled at the front, we formed a train behind Father as he walked up and down the rows of trees. When one caught Father's eye, he stopped and lifted it up. With the tree standing upright, he shook it hard, loosening the braches and freeing them of snow. Handing it to James, Father circled around it a few times. If it had a flaw, Father squinted, wrinkled his nose, and then shook his head no. James dropped the tree back on its ledge, and our train moved on.

It didn't take long for Father's quest for perfection to frustrate me. So what if the tree was flawed. Couldn't we just get one and head back home? I wanted it decorated and glowing in our picture window. I wanted our house to look like everyone else's. I wanted our family to start Christmas.

Father finally picked a tree worthy of his ideal, and he paid the clerk while I danced with excitement. He dropped the tree on top of the sled and its branches shook like a big wet dog. He picked Brian and Nora up and set them on either side of the prickly branches.

The sun had set when we headed away from the light of the shopping center into the darkness of George Mason Drive. The deep snow now covered the yards, the street, and the median, meshing them all together.

It started to snow again and the world around us came to a peaceful halt. The only sounds were the swish of our sled and the gentle crunch of our feet on the freshly fallen snow. Our voices traveled into the night without anything to bounce them back. At every streetlight, I tilted my head back as far as I could and watched the perfect little flakes as they floated from the sky. I tried to keep my eyes wide open so the flakes could gently sting my eyeballs.

The silence mixed with the falling snow made me feel like I lived in a fairytale. This wasn't Virginia, but a land far away. The fluffy flakes were stars falling to earth. Father was a wonderful, caring man, the way fathers are supposed to be. My brothers and sisters were safe and secure on a mighty adventure. Mother was home humming Christmas carols while stirring a pot of warm hot chocolate. Every few minutes glancing out the window for the first signs of our safe return.

The snow lit up Father and James as they trudged side-by-side, leaning forward slightly as if pushed by a strong wind. The heavy sled and their boots were sinking deep into the snow. The night was so perfect, I prayed they wouldn't get tired and give up. That nothing would go wrong. More streetlights came up and my fairytale went on.

At home, Mother's smiling face encouraged me when she opened the back door. She helped me remove my mittens and unwind my wet scarf. So far the night had been perfect. But it was late and Father still had to string up the tree and put on the lights before the ornaments got hung. I wanted to hurry up and decorate the tree before his mood changed.

Mother helped Brian and Nora peel off their layers of wet clothing. The box of Nestlé's Quick sat on the counter. The smell of hot chocolate simmering on the stove filled the kitchen. Mother quickly poured it into the five mugs lined up on the counter. I wrapped my freezing hands around the warm cup and took a big whiff of the steamy chocolate. My fingers tingled as the heat thawed them out.

While we were gone, Mother had brought the ornament boxes down from the attic and stacked the trays of glass bulbs all over the living room. She'd begun the process of checking each light strand for burned out bulbs. She'd cleared the space in front of the picture window for us to present our tree to the neighborhood.

At times like these, Father was unpredictable. At any moment, something could set him off, and he'd stop everything. If he got mad and yelled at Mother, she'd retreat to her room. But that night, nothing happened. In fact, he became lively, rubbing the top of Brian's head, calling Sheila his "first mate," and humming "God Rest Ye Merry Gentlemen."

With patience, Father sat cross-legged on the floor and put together the green and red tree stand. A few minutes later, he and James pushed open the kitchen door, dragging the tree behind them. They carried it into the living room and dropped it on its side. With a hammer, Father rammed the prongs of the tree stand into the bottom of the trunk. The noise rang through the house like a gong signaling the arrival of Christmas. With the tree standing upright, James held it while the rest of us stood back staring at its beautiful naked branches.

"Turn it to the right," Father said.

James twisted the tree around, keeping his eye on Father.

Mother, with her arms folded across her chest, leaned against the wall. James kept twisting the tree while Father walked around, checking it on all sides. I didn't understand why he had to be so picky. Every angle looked the same to me.

Finally Father said, "Stop right there. That's perfect."

James stood stiff, holding the tree while Father crawled underneath and tightened the screws around the trunk.

Father stood up and picked up his pipe from the ashtray on his desk. He dipped the bowl into a foil bag of tobacco and used the side of the package to pack it down. His lighter clicked as he tossed back the lid with his thumb. Then he hovered the flame over the top and sucked it down into the tobacco. Three short puffs later, the bowl glowed bright red.

While holding his pipe close to his mouth, he glanced around the room. His chin went out, pushing up his lower lip. He nodded his head slightly and puffed out his chest, as if he himself had made that tree grow.

Father set the glowing pipe back in the ashtray and took his old seaman's sewing kit out of the bottom drawer of his desk. From a wooden spool, he pulled off a long piece of thick green thread and snipped it with the tiny scissors from the kit.

Tying the thread around one of the sagging bottom branches, he wove it through to the top of the tree pulling the stray branch up off the floor. He then tied the other end around a top branch. He did this until the tree was worthy of his idea of perfection. His obsession with the placement of each branch became unbearable. I still feared the night would end before we got our presents. I wanted him to hurry, because the sooner we got the ornaments hung, the less chance there was for him to start trouble.

With the tree tied up, Father began the boring process of putting on the lights. Mother stood back monitoring the process. When lights of the same color were too close together, she'd patiently rearrange them. She made sure the lights facing the street were just as perfect as the ones facing our living room.

After the lights came our turn to help. All night I had stared at the red and green glass bulbs in their little cubbies. They looked so safe surrounded by their thin cardboard dividers. I wanted to play with them but feared they'd break.

When we came to the box with Sheila's little angel, all decorating stopped. Born premature on December 19th, Sheila stayed in the hospital through her first Christmas. On Christmas day, the nurses hung the ceramic angel on her bassinette. Every year to celebrate Sheila's survival, Father made us watch as he lifted her up so she could hang her angel high on the tree. I guess it satisfied some vision he had of himself—the dutiful father and the adoring daughter. His one moment of glory on December 24th, to balance the horror of the rest of the year's days.

That year, none of my worst fears came true. We finished decorating the tree and Mother and Father sent us to our rooms to wait for the presents. With our doors shut tight, we gathered around to listen as the attic stairs opened. We heard the steps creak under Father's weight and the shuffling of boxes over our heads. Then the steps moaned as he came back down.

Standing halfway down the ladder he hollered, "The reindeer are up there and they're pooping in the attic."

We girls giggled. Brian and James' laughed out loud. Father climbed up and down the stairs for what seemed like hours.

The banging stopped and the house grew quiet. We sat huddled by the door, waiting for Father's signal. Then we heard it, the soulful sound of his clarinet announcing everything was ready. We threw open the doors and made a mad dash for the stairs, elbowing each other on the way down. We piled into the living room while Father stood next to the tree, still playing his clarinet.

Our presents weren't under the tree, but spread in five little piles all over the room. Mine were heaped on the small chair we called the "sleeping chair," because it pulled out into a narrow bed. I knelt down and started to open the one on top. Excited, I went around the room, showing everyone my new jigsaw puzzle.

All night I was torn between looking at my brothers and

sisters' gifts and playing with my own. Every time I looked at Mother, she smiled. Father *ooohed* and *ahhed* over all our gifts. Everything about that day seemed "normal." Father and Mother worked together, and our happiness mattered. Why couldn't it be like this all the time? Why didn't Father see how much our lives would be better if he were nice?

The snow stayed for the rest of the Christmas vacation. When Father shoveled off the sidewalk, it made a wall of snow around the yard. The snow made the street seem quieter, the neighborhood more beautiful, our house warmer. I played in the yard until my fingers froze. When I came in, Mother let me make hot chocolate.

On New Year's Eve just before midnight, Father handed out our instruments. James unpacked his trumpet and the rest of us got our recorders. When midnight came, we followed Father onto our front porch. As if on queue, every neighbor came out too, and started to make noise. Some people yelled, some set off firecrackers. But not us, we lined up and Father, our conductor, said, "Ah, one, and ah two." And like the amateurs we were, we played "Olde Lang Syne."

When it came time to return to school, I packed all my presents in a brown paper bag and set it next to my chair until show and tell. When the teacher asked what we got for Christmas, my hand was the first one up. I pulled out my new puzzle and showed it to the class. Then one by one, I pulled out each of my gifts. When I finished, the teacher asked who else had something. A boy raised his hand and said, "I got a new bike." Another raised his hand with his new watch sparkling on his wrist.

I felt sick to my stomach. Compared to a bicycle, my stuff was dime store junk. I never got a bike or a watch. Neither did my brothers and sisters. While Father got himself fancy clothes and cars, he bought us cheap presents from the trays at Bruce's Variety Store.

The magic of Christmas wore off when I got to school. That Christmas, I almost believed in Santa Claus. Father seemed so normal, the way I imagined fathers should be. He almost convinced me he cared when he cursed the reindeer poop. The clarinet sounded so sweet.

But after show and tell, I decided I could never believe in Santa Claus or fairy tales. They were nothing more than tricks to get me to believe in things that weren't real. Father had used Christmas to get me to believe he was a good father. But I learned the truth. If he really cared, he'd be nice to us all the time, not just on one day. Or, at the very least, Al would have come home.

Mother never said much that Christmas. I never heard her go up and down the attic stairs. It was all Father's show. She made us hot chocolate and quietly helped us decorate the tree. Reminding me to put one strand of tinsel on at a time. No clumps of the silvery spaghetti allowed. I remember her sitting on the sofa, smiling as we opened our presents. She seemed to be happy. But now I'm not so sure. Maybe all she wanted was to believe in the fairytale too.

That year, I gave up all hope of ever being a normal family. I decided it was Father's fault. He was the strongest, and he made us live the way he wanted to live. And we only had good times when he wanted them. All the stories were his to tell. For me, that Christmas changed everything. I now knew I didn't have to listen to his fairytales. And I didn't have to believe the stories that weren't true.

MADNESS

OUR WORLD STARTED AND ENDED with my father's idea of order. Yet, in his quest for organization, he created chaos. Now he wanted the house clean, and he wanted it done right! His younger brother, Fred, and his family were coming to visit from Delaware. Mother didn't care. After sixteen years, she'd given up trying to please father. She spent her days sitting around reading newspapers and magazines. And, as if to goad him, she clipped out articles and added them to the piles of junk she kept spread all over the house. Father, in a rage, took matters into his own hands.

The argument started early in the morning. For once Father had a point, the house was a disaster. The piles of dirty clothes on the kitchen floor blocked access to the washer and dryer. The stack of dishes in the sink towered all the way to the faucet. Whoever played rummy last had left the cards scattered across the living room floor. Someone started a jigsaw puzzle in the dining room and the pieces had fallen under the table. Piles of the magazines and newspapers Mother constantly saved were stacked knee-high in every corner of the house. It had been weeks since any surface tasted soap.

Every time Father decided to clean, it led to a fight. Several months before, he and Mother battled over the best way to defrost the freezer. A large chunk of ice had collected around the door, blocking it from closing tightly. Mother wanted to turn it off and let it melt on its own, but Father had a better idea. After a few minutes of bickering, he stormed out to the shed and came back with a blowtorch.

He opened the valve and placed his lighter in front of the pipe. The canister growled as the bluish red flame rushed out.

"Edmund! You'll ruin the freezer with that thing," Mother scolded as the oily smell of the propane filled the kitchen. But Father ignored her and began waving the flame over the thick chunk of ice around the seal.

When the ice began to melt all over the kitchen floor, Mother shouted, "Edmund, you're making a mess." She picked up a dirty towel from the laundry heap and began sopping up the puddle of water.

"Get out of my way," Father said, pushing her aside.

When the seal caught fire, Mother threw down the towel, and on her way out through the kitchen door, she said, "Now you've ruined it!" Her footsteps creaked on the stairs and a few seconds later, her bedroom door slammed.

Sheila and I gathered around giggling at the sight of Father waving the flame over the ice. When he finished, Father stood back and folded his arms across his chest. Ignoring the big black mark the flame left on the inside of the door he opened and shut it several times, admiring how well it now closed. Sheila grabbed another towel and finished cleaning up the water.

But this day, I refused to think about cleaning the house. From the moment their argument woke me, the bright sunshine had begged me to come outside. Before I'd even taken off my pajamas, I slid the bedroom window up, stuck my head out, and took a deep breath of the unusually hot spring air. "It's like a summer day," I said, loud enough to wake Sheila and Nora.

"Come on Sheila, get up. It's Saturday. Let's go downstairs and make some pancakes."

Sheila sat up and rubbed her eyes. Nora started to stir. We charged down the stairs, and headed for the kitchen. But Mother and Father's argument kept us from opening the door.

"Fred and Peg are coming tomorrow," Father snarled. "And just look at this pig sty."

"Well if you had let Daddy help buy us a bigger house, we wouldn't have this problem," Mother snapped back.

"It will be a cold day in hell before I take a goddamn dime from your parents. If you only acted more like a mother instead of sitting around on your fat arse …"

So far, the day wasn't shaping up at all the way I planned. Didn't Father realize we never cleaned our house? I sat down at the dining room table and tried to ignore their fight. Sheila sat next to me and we waited.

Their voices grew until Mother had enough. She came charging through the swinging kitchen door and ran up the stairs. Father followed right behind her into the living room and sat down at his desk. He lit his pipe with the usual three short puffs and stared at the wall. The bottle of vodka came out of the bottom drawer. Discreetly, he filled a small glass to the top. The glass met his lips and he threw back his head drinking it all down in one gulp. His lips smacked together, his tongue clicked off the roof of his mouth and he let out a long, "ahhhh." Still staring straight ahead, he took three more puffs of his pipe.

While keeping an eye on him, I began to devise a way to escape outside. If I skipped breakfast, slipped out the back door, and played quietly in the yard, Father would forget all about me. But before I could scram, his back straightened. He set his pipe in the ashtray and pushed out his chair, bumping the legs across the uneven pieces of the hardwood floor. Stretching, he grabbed his web belt and pulled up his trousers. When he headed for the stairs, I crossed my fingers behind my back, hoping he'd stay away from Mother.

In the upstairs hall, the hinges on the pull-down attic stairs creaked and the ladder banged as it hit the floor. I ran to the top of the stairs just as Father disappeared into the ceiling. Mother opened her door and stood still, listening to the sound of Father's footsteps over her head. Father hollered down, "Goddammit, Josephine, I've had it with all this crap. I'm throwing everything out."

Mother bit her lip, and her eyes flared. She stormed to the

My Mother's Song

foot of the ladder and yelled up into the attic, "If you throw away any of my magazines, when I die, I'll come back to haunt you!" Then she went back into her room and slammed the door.

Hmm, that's an appealing thought. Mother haunting Father seemed like justice. I imagined her as a fluffy white ghost without any feet, wearing a long flowing dress. Everywhere Father went she followed, flying in little circles around his head. I imagined him swatting at her, but his hand going right through her body. I imagined him scared to death, trying to get away from her. I almost wanted it to come true, until I realized Mother would have to die.

Piles of clothes came flying down the attic stairs. Father looked through the hole and said to me, "Get your brothers and sisters and take this junk to the side yard." Sheila stepped out of our bedroom and she and I each gathered an armful of old clothes and made our way downstairs and out the back door. Still holding the clothes, we stood there in the middle of the side yard, looking at each other. Then I shrugged and we both emptied our arms, dropping everything into a heap on the grass.

When we returned to the upstairs hall, the junk pile at the bottom of the ladder had grown. Now old books, toys, and Christmas decorations blocked the hallway. On top sat the old plastic wreath we hung on our front door every Christmas. Its glitter had brushed off into the clothes and they sparkled in the sunlight now pouring through our open bedroom door. I picked up the wreath and stuck it through my arm, pushing it up to my bicep. I scooped up another pile of clothes and trudged downstairs, getting glitter all over the front of my dress. Sheila followed me, carrying a stack of books that smelled like mildew. Together we added our stuff to the top of the growing pile in the yard.

Nora and Brian worked as a team, picking up one or two items and trying to hurry them outside. Father hollered down the stairs to James, "I want all that crap cleaned up now."

"Everyone's helping Father," James said trying to calm him

down. But I knew he was really trying to figure out Father's next move. I knew he feared something might go wrong.

Nervously, James kept organizing the pile at the foot of the stairs while handing us our next loads. Every few minutes, he glanced up the ladder. Like bombs exploding in the attic, more junk came flying through the hole. Father's footsteps banged across the ceiling over the boys' room, followed by loud scratching noises as he slid around more boxes.

When Father finally came down the ladder, beads of sweat ran down his forehead and trickled through his beard. The underarms of his white tee shirt were soaking wet. He brushed flakes of insulation off his pants, then he bent over and scooped up an armful of the remaining junk on the floor. James folded up the attic stairs and slammed them shut. The five of us picked up the rest of the stuff and followed father out to the side yard.

I dropped the last bits of junk on the now huge pile. Father went all around the edges of the heap, scooping stuff up, making the pile higher and higher. In all the shuffling, the Christmas wreath slid down right in front of my feet. Mother's threat to haunt Father worked, because none of her magazines ended up in the yard.

As if he didn't know what to do next, Father paced back and forth, staring at the pile of junk. He covered his mouth and slowly pulled his hand down across the whiskers of his chin. With one of his unfiltered Camels dangling in his lips, he dug deep in his pocket and pulled out his silver lighter. He threw back the lid, clicked on the flame, and sucked in a deep draw. The corners of his mouth went down and he curled in his lips, exposing his two protruding front teeth. He squinted as smoke ran out his nose and mouth, the smoke that smelled just like him.

In a flash, he perked up and briskly walked through the gate into the backyard. A few seconds later, he returned, carrying a shiny red can of gasoline. He tossed the open can forward and little arches of the clear gas floated up and landed on the pile. With every thrust, the smell of gas got stronger and stronger.

When the can was empty, he turned it upside down and shook out the last few drops. Then he tossed it behind him and pulled out his lighter.

Picking up an old pair of navy blue shorts, Father waved the flame underneath the them and they immediately caught on fire. Casually, he flung them down on top of the pile then took a few steps backwards.

With a loud, *whhooosh,* all the junk burst into flames. For several minutes, we stood there in a trance, mesmerized by the fire. It burned through the cotton clothing, shrinking each piece into little handfuls of ashes. As the books burned, they opened up, and the pages curled in sending a spiral of little sparks into the sky. If I closed my eyes, it smelled like we were outside on a spring day, burning our leaves.

As the fire came closer and closer to the plastic wreath, the realization of what Father was doing hit me. Stop! I didn't want anything else to burn. Especially the cheap plastic wreath. I liked its fake walnuts and glitter, and the holly leaves almost looked real. Every year right after Thanksgiving, Mother hung it on our door. To me, it symbolized the start of the holiday season. I admit, it no longer looked its best, but it represented something special to me and I didn't want it destroyed. I wanted to reach over and rescue that wreath, but I didn't dare.

The fire latched onto one side of the wreath and my nostrils filled with the putrid smell of burning plastic. As it began to melt, the fire hissed and reduced the fake pine boughs to a dark green liquid that began to drip. The heat caused the small plastic walnuts to cave in and bubble into puddles of dark brown gook.

Fury began to swell in my chest. Like a rope with many strands, it twisted around my knot and then wrenched it tight. All I could think about was how much I liked that stupid wreath. And how, in some sordid way, my Father was burning Christmas.

As the fire began to die down, smugness came over Father.

He seemed pleased with himself like he'd accomplished a heroic deed. With the fire still smoldering, I went inside.

For the rest of the day I couldn't stop thinking about that wreath. When I closed my eyes, all I could see were the caved-in bubbling walnuts. Even though it was April, I wanted to bring it back and put it on our front door. How could Father not know how much it meant to me? How could he be so reckless with the things the rest of us loved?

Back inside the house, Father gathered us together in the kitchen and ordered us to take all the dirty laundry out to the backyard. Without any questions, we quickly obeyed. I picked up an armful of musty smelling towels and took them outside and dumped them over the back porch railing. Nora and Brian mimicked me, adding their clothes to the pile. Father told Sheila and me to wash all the dishes and put them away.

I took my time filling the sink with soapy water. I slowly ran the rag over the plates, and Sheila rinsed them under the running faucet. Neither one of us were in a hurry to see what Father wanted done next.

Convinced that Father's sole motivation was to upset the family, I didn't want to make him mad. As a kid, I coped by ignoring any dread or fear that crept in. After watching the wreath burn, I couldn't let the knot in my chest tighten any further, nor could I let it begin to unravel. Somehow, focusing on my knot held me together.

Late in the afternoon, without fixing us anything to eat, Father changed into clean clothes and left. Mother came down, and she and James talked quietly on the sofa. Sheila and I made some macaroni and cheese for dinner. At some point, probably very late, we all obeyed James and went to bed.

I don't know how long I'd been asleep before James's voice woke me up. At first I thought it was a dream.

"Father, please, just go back downstairs and leave her alone."

But my eyes were open and the hall light streamed through

my open bedroom door. From the darkness of my room, the bright light looked like a movie playing just outside my door. In the hall stood my father, drunk, swaying back and forth with a gun in his hand. In front of the barrel, stood my brother James.

Father mumbled something I couldn't hear. From the angle of my bed, I couldn't see his face, but I could tell he didn't have a tight grip on the gun. Sobbing, James just kept pleading, "Come on, Father," he begged. "Please, go back downstairs and leave Mother alone."

Cocking his head to the side Father seemed to be considering James's plea. He lowered the gun slightly but kept it pointed at him. Drunkenly, he swayed side to side then lowered his arm and walked down the stairs, the clump of his heavy boots growing distant on the hardwood steps.

Even though I was almost eleven, I never thought of James as a thirteen-year-old. The three years between us seemed more like ten. To me, James was more than a brother; he was our protector, our keeper of peace, the one trying to keep everything safe. Feeling he had Father under control, I rolled over in the dark and waited for the sun to come up. As my mind wandered to thoughts of the following day, school, and my friends, I fell back asleep.

Before I knew it, bright sunlight burned through my eyelids. Lying on my back, I stretched my arms over my head. Then I rubbed my face and picked the sleep from my eyes. Without using the ladder, I jumped off the top bunk and landed on the floor with a loud thud. Usually the first one up, I was surprised to find my sisters' beds empty. I remembered something happening the night before, but the images seemed so vague it must have been a dream. Adding my nightgown to the clutter on my bed, I stepped into the sundress I'd worn the day before and tried to wipe off the few remaining pieces of glitter.

There were no voices chattering as I skipped every other step on my way downstairs. On Sunday, I usually woke to the smell of bacon and the sound of dishes banging in the kitchen. But that day, there were no smells or sounds coming from inside the house. I wandered through the empty living room and kicked open the swinging kitchen door, expecting to find everyone there. But the room was empty and the backdoor wide open.

The spring on the wooden screen door creaked as I pushed it out and let it bang hard behind me. When I didn't hear Mother customary, "Don't slam the door!" I began to wonder if the "movie" from the night before was real. Squinting in the bright sunlight, I walked out the back gate and around to the front of the house.

There in the middle of the front yard stood James and Sheila watching Father as he tried to place a tall wooden ladder against the house. Brian and Nora, freed from the backyard, were sitting in the grass. Unable to hold the ladder still, Father stared straight up while taking little steps to the left and right in an attempt to gain his balance.

After several minutes of jostling, the ladder banged against the brick and Father tried to stabilize it without falling over. He stepped back about ten feet and intently looked up and down the ladder as if it were difficult to see. Then, with both hands firmly on the edges of the ladder, he placed his right foot on the first rung. But when he lifted his left foot, his body pulled to the right and he started to sway, pulling the ladder with him.

With both feet planted on the ground, he took a deep breath and again, looked up and down the ladder. Pausing for a second to gain strength, he grabbed the edges and pulled the ladder further away from the house. With difficulty, he got his right foot on the first rung, but like before, when he lifted his left, he and the ladder began to fall.

At the time, Father did so many odd things, the sight of him at 6:00 in the morning, trying to place a ladder against the house, didn't alarm me. Part of me wondered if he planned to wash the windows, and part of me wondered if he just wanted to "get Mother's goat." At first, neither one seemed scary, so I sat down and continued watching the show.

Frustrated, Father turned around and looked at us. With his brows pulled tightly together, he squinted as though he couldn't figure out who we were. Methodically, he glared at each one of us until his eyes rested on Sheila. "Sheila, come here," he slurred. "Climb up the ladder and look in the window. Tell me if there's a man in the room with *her*."

A pang of jealously went through me. I wanted to climb the ladder, but Father never asked me to do anything. I didn't want to spy on Mother, but climbing the ladder looked like fun. Besides, we all knew Mother didn't have a man in her room. But if Father did ask me to climb the ladder, and I did see another man, I wouldn't feel guilty about lying. I would just tell him Mother was all alone.

Father picked Sheila up and set her part of the way up the ladder. Gingerly, she grabbed the edges, and stretched her short legs to reach the next step. When she managed to pull herself up and get her other foot on the rung, she stopped and looked down at Father, as if hoping he'd tell her to come down. With her red hair blowing in the breeze, she again lifted her right leg, brought up the other, then looked down at Father.

Just before Sheila reached the top, Mother appeared behind the closed window. The fear on her face made the blood rush to my head. Suddenly, my mind raced to catch up with what was going on.

"I think it's time for you guys to go inside," James barked. But I froze, staring at Father, then back at Sheila, then over at James.

For the first time that morning, fear swept over me, and I began to add up all the events of the day before. The early morning fight, the fire, and the movie in the hall. I just knew something really bad was happening. That this fight could not be ignored, that someone might get hurt this time.

Now afraid Sheila might fall, I held my breath until she reached Mother's bedroom window. Slowly with one hand, she let go of the ladder, cupped it around her eyes, and leaned in close to the glass. After staring inside for a few moments, she carefully grabbed the edge of the ladder, turned around and looked down at Father. "There's no one there but Mother."

"Look again!" he demanded. "Are you sure?"

James seemed torn between keeping an eye on Father and Sheila and telling us to go back inside.

"Come on you guys, get back inside," he said. But, I still couldn't move or take my eyes off what was happening.

Nervously, Sheila cupped her hand again and leaned toward the glass and peered in the window. Again she turned around and looked down at Father. "There's no one else there."

Father grunted and stared at her in disbelief. With a look of determination, he turned and walked through the side yard and disappeared through the gate, leaving Sheila alone at the top of the ladder.

Part of me wanted to stay and help Sheila, but the other part wanted to keep an eye on Father. Maybe if I could figure out what he planned to do, I could stop him. As Sheila made her way down the ladder, I followed Father to the shed in the back yard.

Keeping my distance, I stood outside the shed as Father banged around inside. With a sledgehammer in one hand and a brace and bit drill in the other, his body filled the doorway on his way out. Tucked in his belt, was the big Luger.

I followed him through the backdoor and up the stairs to the locked door leading to Mother's room. Still too drunk to function, he got on his knees and placed the sharp tip of the drill bit into the wood by the doorknob. With his palm firmly on the end of the drill, he slowly turned the crank handle. In resistance, the wood groaned and cracked as the bit plunged slowly into the wood. Small curly shavings that smelled like fresh two-by-fours, pushed out. They spun around, getting longer and longer, until they broke off and fell to the floor.

Methodically, Father repeated the process until he had six neat holes, the same distance from each other, all around the doorknob. When he finished, he set the drill on the floor by the top of the stairs and picked up the sledgehammer. Staggering back to the door he tried to lift the sledgehammer over his head, but in his drunkenness, its weight nearly dragged him over.

On his second try, he didn't try to raise the sledgehammer as high. He grasped it with both hands and lifted it level with his shoulders. With his whole body, he lurched forward and smashed it against the wooden door. The wood splintered like a tree giving way to an axe. The door flew open and slammed against the wall.

At the first pop of the gun, my mind slammed shut. By the second shot, I was already downstairs.

FATHER DIES

HAVING FEARED FATHER WOULD KILL Mother, James stood at the top of the stairs watching everything spiral out of control. The night before, after we went to bed, he had stayed up, waiting for Father to come home. He hoped to calm him down, to talk him into leaving Mother alone. But Father returned drunk and just as mad.

In Father's absence, Mother and James came up with a plan. The wall between her bedroom and the boys' room would allow them to communicate. Afraid of being overheard, Mother told James not to talk, but to scratch on the wall if Father had a gun. In the middle of the night, while Father paced the living room holding his Luger, James snuck up the stairs and gave Mother the warning.

All night Mother's brilliant analytical mind had played out every possible scenario. She knew that, eventually, Father would try to break down the door. She knew if he succeeded in killing her, the trauma would jolt him out of his drunken madness. With her dead, he'd most likely want to kill himself, but she feared he'd kill us too. His madness might convince him we'd all be better off dead. Mother already felt dead, but she couldn't bear the thought of her kids dying too.

Trying to think of every possible angle, she came up with the second scenario. If he got through the door, hopefully he'd be too drunk to pull his gun, and she'd be able to fire first. She knew her .22 was no match for his Luger, but she was sober. Perhaps she could do some damage. Incapacitate him enough to get away with us kids.

She banked on the hope that if Father got through the door, he'd be moving slowly. She prayed James did everything they talked about—kept the rest of us downstairs and away from the door

And she prayed she wouldn't be too afraid to shoot. But her worst fear was she'd miss, and somehow hit one of her children.

A short five-foot hallway ran from the door into the bedroom. Aware the distance gave her an advantage, Mother positioned herself in a corner, knowing the two by fours behind the sheetrock formed a barrier against incoming bullets.

When Father started drilling, she stood watching the tip of the drill bit plow through the thick door. She heard every grind of the coiled metal tearing into the hard wood. She knew this was the end and she had to do something.

She jumped at the sound of the sledgehammer. When the door come flying toward her, she didn't wait to see Father's face. Instinct kicked in, and took her back to the firing range at TSCW. Only this time, she closed her eyes, and the first pop startled her. The sound of Father's voice sent a chill up her spine, "Jesus Christ!" Then another pop. "I can't believe she's shooting at me." Then pop, pop, pop.

Her head throbbed like she'd been punched. The sharp piercing ring in her ears blocked out any other sound. The smell of gunpowder filled her nostrils as she opened her eyes. Her hands shook and her heart raced like wild horses galloping over her. She looked down the hallway but didn't see him there. She wondered if she'd completely missed him. Or maybe imagined the whole thing.

But the heavy door swung on its last hinge. The curly wood shavings were scattered across the floor.

Trying to slow her mind down in order to focus, she took several deep breaths. Mentally, she counted the shots. She'd only fired five.

Relieved to have one remaining, she slowly made her way past the door and down the hallway. As she walked toward the boys' room, she saw the tips of Father's boots sticking out of the doorway. She peeked around the corner and saw him on the floor, lying on his side with his back to the door. His legs pulled up to his chest.

Thinking it was a trap, she placed her left hand over the gun and grabbed it firmly with both hands to steady her nerves. Like a police officer, she placed her body close to the wall and tiptoed silently through the door.

He didn't move, but she couldn't see his hands or face. For all she knew, he still had his gun. Slowly, she stepped into the room and stood in shock over his lifeless body, grateful to not have to look at his face. A small trickle of blood crept out from under his back. At least she'd hit him once. She tightened her grip on the gun; still not convinced he was dead.

Just then, he flinched. From his head to his toes, his body shuddered. Expecting him to jump up and say "Gotcha," she released her last shot into his back. The impact of the bullet shook him one last time. Then his body went limp. He didn't move and she knew he was dead.

Pacing back and forth she kept thinking, "What do I do now?" Still gripping the gun she heard screams she knew were Sheila's.

Not wanting us to see the gun, she walked back into the bedroom and set it high on the bookshelf. It took several moments for her stiff hands to uncurl and release the gun. It landed on the shelf with a thud. Her fingers buzzed, and now the whole upstairs smelled of gunpowder.

When she tried to walk, her legs felt like rubber. Her body functioned ten seconds behind her brain. She made a quick glance at Father's body then headed down the hallway, but all she saw was the growing puddle of blood. Relieved none of her children were nearby, she hurried down the stairs.

The minute Mother stepped off the bottom step, she quickly did a head count like we were at the grocery store. She let out a deep breath then scooped up Sheila, who had been standing in the middle of the living room with her hands by her sides and her mouth wide open. Over and over she'd been screaming at the top of her lungs until she ran out of breath. Then she frantically gulped in more air and screamed again. With Sheila on her lap, Mother sat down at Father's desk.

"Shush, shush, shush, it will be all right," she said, rocking her back and forth.

But Sheila's face got redder and redder, she just kept on screaming. Brian cried in hiccupping outbursts. Nora cried like she knew something really horrible had happened but didn't understand what. James wept the way a grown man cries. That gut-wrenching kind of sobbing when an adult knows life has just become severely damaged.

But me, I stood behind them all, feeling nothing but relief. No sadness and no fear. Just a sense of gratitude toward Mother for protecting us. My worst fear had come true, and now that he was gone, it didn't seem so bad.

Sheila's screams became whimpers, and Mother set her down and let out an exhausted sigh. With her elbows on the desk, she rested her forehead on the tips of her fingers and began to sob. The only noise she made came from her occasional sniffles. But her shoulders went up and down and tears steadily dripped off her chin and formed little puddles on top of the desk.

Mother's sadness came over me like a heavy quilt. My chest tightened, but still no tears came out. Somehow I knew the sadness would be more than my young heart could bear. That giving in to it would make my chest explode and my knot unwind, turning me into a crazed child, who couldn't stop screaming.

Inside my mind, two people emerged. One a child, and the other an adult. The child held her breath while the adult kept saying, "It's okay. Don't cry. He's gone and he'll never come back. Mother will be okay. When this is over, everything is going to be better."

Time went in slow motion. After what seemed like an hour, Mother finally spoke in a monotone I barely recognized, "I need to call the police." I'm not sure what I thought she should have done, but calling the police never occurred to me. Just the thought of it made me want to jump across the room and rip the phone off the wall. I wanted to scream, "No! We don't need them! What did they ever do for us?" But I had lost control of my body; nothing felt real, I felt like I was watching myself in a dream.

But Mother was serious. In slow motion, she picked up the receiver, placed her finger in the hole, and dialed the first number. The wheel rattled and it took forever to wind back down before she dialed again. I kept thinking, hoping, and praying she would stop. Maybe come to her senses and think of a new plan. But she didn't, she just kept dialing. And I kept staring at wheel as it wound back down.

Giving no introduction, Mother's voice came out in that strange monotone, "I'm Mrs. Gibson, at 1202 South Buchanan Street, and I would like to see an officer." Then she paused, "Oh, it's my husband again."

Within minutes, off in the distance, sirens began to wail. The sound grew louder and louder, like a swirling bull's eye that zeroed in on our house. I wanted to hide when the police car, with its lights flashing, pulled up. Mother opened the front door to two officers standing on our porch. Treating them like neighbors coming to visit, she pushed out the screen and said, "Come on in."

The taller officer, with his hands resting on the gun belt around his waist, asked, "What's the trouble, ma'am?"

Mother took a deep breath and, with a puzzled look, slowly said, "It's my husband."

The shorter officer with his right hand on the handle of his pistol, looked ready to draw. "Where is he?"

"Oh," Mother said, then she paused. "He's upstairs, dead."

Both officers went into action. The short one raised his eyebrows and, with his hand still on his pistol, ran up the stairs. The tall one quickly looked around the room. In an overly friendly voice he said, "Come here, guys," motioning with his hand. "I need all of you to go in the backyard and try not to think about what happened."

Mother walked back to the desk and plopped her heavy body into the chair. She seemed confused to no longer have control of the situation. I didn't want to leave. I didn't want to turn my back on Mother and walk away. But I followed James to the backyard.

Once outside, I tried to think of something to say to break the tension, but no words formed in my mind. I could only think in pictures. The ladder. The drill. James's face. The curly wood shavings. Father, swaying back and forth. Nothing but pictures. I wanted to do what the officer said and not think of what happened, but the images would not go away.

Again I heard a siren from far away, whining closer and closer, again announcing our tragedy. Broadcasting to our neighbors to come take a look. Through a crack in the fence, I watched until the ambulance pulled up in front of our house.

On the curb across the street, a crowd had already gathered. Some still in bathrobes, with uncombed hair. They all stared at our house as if they could see through the brick, see Mother with the police and see the body upstairs.

Turning away from the fence, I went back to pretending it was a normal day. I tried not thinking about Mother alone in the house with the police. I tried to swing on the pull-up bar. With the edge of my hand, I carved out narrow roads in the gravel for Brian's cars. I tried to get his attention, to get him to come and look, but he just wandered around in a daze.

Standing up, I brushed the dirt off my knees and walked over next to Sheila. She stood by the fence with her head down, staring at the ground. I leaned down to look her in the eye. "Come on, Sheila, come see my roads. Do you want to help me make some more?" But my words bounced off her blank face.

James stood next to the gate, watching us. His eyes moved, but they seemed detached from his brain. The seriousness in his gaze made my chest tighten. Wanting him to smile, I stared straight at him and tried to think of something funny to say. I wanted the day to end, and time to jump to next week. Because maybe by then my family wouldn't hurt anymore.

It seemed like I was the only one alive and all my siblings were zombies. James and Sheila with their blank stares. Nora and Brian still in childish bewilderment. But I still felt nothing but that strange, sweet-tasting relief. Already, I had begun to imagine the better lives we'd have without Father.

After failing to wake my siblings, my curiosity started to bubble. I couldn't stop wondering what the police and Mother were doing inside the house. Besides, everything was starting to seem too unreal. Like I'd dreamed it all and Father wasn't really upstairs dead on the floor. Maybe, I could sneak back inside to see the body before they took it away. Something had to be done to quench my burning desire for proof of my father's death. So I began to scheme.

For the next hour, I wandered from my tangled roads to the open back door. The swinging kitchen door was propped-open giving me a clear view into the living room. Mother still sat at Father's desk with her back to me. But I couldn't hear anything through the screen.

Mother looked so alone sitting there by herself. I wanted to be bigger so I could run inside and sit down next to her. I wanted to tell her it was okay she shot my father, that I thought he got what he deserved.

When one of the officers left, I got my chance to get back inside. The remaining policeman stood leaning over Mother with his hand on her shoulder. Mother still sat in the same position at Father's desk. My opportunity had arrived.

I waited several minutes and worked up the nerve to slip open the screen door. On my tippy toes, pressed against the wall, I passed Mother and the officer and went up the stairs. Strong rays of sunlight poured into the hallway from the window in our bedroom, revealing a slight layer of smoke. The whole upstairs smelled like someone set off an entire package of fireworks.

My steps slowed as I walked past my bedroom and stood inside the doorway to the boy's room. Just inside the door, Father's body laid curled up in a ball, with his back to the hallway. Thankfully, I couldn't see his face. I wondered if his eyes were open, but was afraid to get any closer to lean over and check.

With both feet flat on the floor, I stood there, stunned to be looking at a dead body, at my own father's dead body. A large pool of blood seeped from underneath his back. His dirty thin grey hair was matted in spots, and I could see the bald spot on the back of his head. My skin crawled and a chill ran through me, causing me to shiver. What was his last thought? Was he sorry now for all the things he did to Mother? As he lay dying, did he regret trying to kill her?

Afraid of getting caught upstairs, I slipped down the steps and peered around the corner into the living room. The officer's body still blocked Mother, with his back to me. I crept by and bolted through the kitchen and back outside. Holding onto the screen door, I closed it without making a sound. Then I stood on the porch, waiting for my heart to stop pounding, surprised James hadn't realized I was gone.

Nora and Brian were playing with my roads, so I joined them, like I'd never left. There I was, on a normal spring day, ignoring the birds chirping in the top of the blackberry tree. Trying to keep from looking at my siblings' pain. Trying to force everything around me to go away. Trying to keep my mind in the backyard.

But my thoughts kept wandering back inside.

Getting restless, I peered through a crack in the fence just in time to see two men in white uniforms pushing a stretcher toward the back of the ambulance. Father's body lay face up, covered by a white sheet. The sheet hid everything except the tips of his ugly brown boots. In one shove, they loaded him into the back of the ambulance. Such a strange ending for such a strange life. And, I wondered why I hated those brown boots.

It was afternoon before the policeman opened the screen door and told us to come inside. My heart sank when I saw the empty chair at Father's desk. Somehow I knew they'd taken her away, but it never dawned on me they'd arrest my mother for murder. For some reason, I figured she'd come home in time to fix us dinner.

I sat down next to Sheila on the sofa. Brian and Nora sat on the other side of her, and we waited. But for what, I wasn't quite sure. I thought about getting up and going into the kitchen for a glass of water but, with the police there, the house no longer seemed like ours. James sat in the sleeping chair, still looking far away. But I didn't even think he could get up and get me a glass of water.

It bothered me the way the policemen kept whispering to each other. What did they have to say that we couldn't hear? They talked with their heads together, then one left for a while. He came back and they whispered some more, then he left again. Years later, I learned they had no place to take us. That they were going door to door, begging someone to take us in. Telling them the only place they had to send us was the Juvenile Detention Center.

Late that afternoon, I held on tight to Nora's hand as we followed the policeman down Buchanan Street toward the cul-de-sac. When we came close to the house with a chain link fence around the front and back yards, Sheila whispered, "I hope they're not taking us to live with the sheriff. His house looks just like a prison."

That thought never occurred to me, so I held my breath until we got completely past the fence. At the very last house on the right, the policeman opened the screen door and knocked. A petite, beautiful, dark-haired woman opened the door. She smiled tenderly and said, "Welcome, welcome. Come in. Make yourselves at home. My name is Mrs. Joseph." She motioned to a man sitting on a sofa. "This is Mr. Joseph, and we're both so glad to have you here."

Mr. Joseph was small like Father, but the similarity ended there. He watched us with his soft brown eyes as we piled into the room. He came over and gently shook our hands. His tenderness loosened, ever so slightly, the knot in my chest.

The officer spoke quietly to Mrs. Joseph then he left. Mrs. Joseph introduced us to her daughter, Laura, who was about the same age as Nora. Timidly, we each told Laura our names. Her eyes followed down the line of the five of us.

All the rooms in the Joseph's house were the same size and in the same place as ours. But instead of stale smoke they smelled like a combination of soap and baked cookies. Their house sat beside a little creek and, without a neighbor and no tall fence, the sun poured through their sheer curtains, flooding the living room in bright yellow light.

Mrs. Joseph fed us peanut butter and jelly sandwiches. After dinner, Mr. and Mrs. Joseph arranged five sleeping bags across their living room floor.

That night, I don't remember talking much as we got dressed for bed. It seemed so weird for all five of us to be spending the night in someone else's house. When it was time to go to bed, Mrs. Joseph held open our sleeping bags while we crawled inside. She said good night and turned out the lights.

Again, I couldn't think in words, only in pictures. Father's body on the stretcher, Mother and the policeman, James's blank stare. They played over and over, like a slide show in my mind.

For a long time, I lay awake in the dark, aware of the strange place. The streetlight crept in around the curtains and cast grey shadows on the walls. My heart beat softly inside my chest. Already I knew the Joseph's house was nothing like ours.

Even though I didn't know them very well, I felt safe. I just knew Mrs. Joseph would take care of us until Mother came home. So far, Father's death was turning out okay. After all, James was right next to me, ready to pick up any broken pieces. Ready to start putting us all back together.

That night I hoped, with Father gone, James could begin to

feel some relief. I hoped his greatest fear had come true and, like me, it didn't seem so bad. But the thing none of us could have known was the worst was yet to come. That Father's death would never leave us.

FATHER'S FUNERAL

THE DAY AFTER THE SHOOTING, I had just sat down on the floor in the Joseph's living room when someone knocked on the door. Mr. Joseph opened it and Mrs. Lane stepped right into their house. Not much had changed about her. She wore her usual outfit, a matching tweed skirt and jacket. And just like the night I first met her, she had a long braid wrapped neatly around her head. But now, she reminded me of a mean Heidi, all grown up.

James walked in from the kitchen while Mrs. Lane was introducing herself to the Josephs. Then she put her arm around James' shoulder and said, "Don't worry, everything will be all right." Her skinny hand patted his back like he was two years old. James stood stiff, his face serious, but confused. I knew I should be polite and get up to greet her, but I refused. Nothing could make me stand and let that woman touch me.

Sheila walked in the room, and Mrs. Lane took her arm from James's shoulder and wrapped it around Sheila, saying the same thing. Sheila too stiffened, until Mrs. Lane let her go. How did she know everything would be all right? Her strange friendship with Father made Mother's blood boil. Mother never had nice things to say about her. What was she up to?

After shaking hands with Mrs. Lane, Mr. and Mrs. Joseph sat down next to each other on the sofa. Still standing, with great authority, Mrs. Lane began to speak. The Josephs became one person against this domineering presence, as they leaned closer together. Already, I felt the Josephs were a barrier between my family and Mrs. Lane. But I wondered if their gentleness would crumble under the control of this female version of my father. I prayed the Josephs would not let Mrs. Lane take us to her creepy house.

After Mrs. Lane finished "comforting" us, James stood next to me and Sheila sat down on the floor. None of us wanted to leave the room. Mrs. Lane talked fast like she feared someone might tell her to shut up. She told the Josephs she'd driven straight over from the jail to pick up some clothes for Mother. She kept trying to reassure us that everything would be all right. The Josephs looked questioningly at her, nodding in all the right places, then they looked at each other then over at us.

In my opinion, Mrs. Lane's presence at the Josephs meant things were going in the wrong direction. And nobody even mentioned what had happened to Mother. Why was Mrs. Lane sticking her nose in our business when Mother had never even liked her? I always had a sneaking suspicion that something wasn't right between Mrs. Lane and my father.

Sitting on the floor, I stared up at Mrs. Lane thinking how different she was from my mother. Mrs. Lane was thin, and Mother overweight. Mrs. Lane wore expensive clothes, and Mother wore cheap housedresses. Mrs. Lane spoke in cold sharp jabs, and Mother spoke calmly and gently. But the biggest difference I saw was Mother had patience, while Mrs. Lane always looked angry.

Why, I wondered, hadn't Father just left us and married her? Clearly, he didn't love Mother. Everything she did made him mad. It seemed to me, since Mrs. Lane was so much like father, they would not have fought as much. Therefore Father wouldn't have beaten her the way he did Mother.

We didn't go to school that whole week. To my disappointment, Mrs. Lane came back. This time she brought us clothes for Father's funeral. She said she picked out the three matching sleeveless blue dresses with thick, ribbed white stripes. Mother must have told her to buy them all alike, since she usually dressed us that way for special occasions.

Then, a couple days before the funeral, Sheila and I were playing outside when Mrs. Joseph called us in. "There's someone here to see you," she said with excitement. I ran through the front door and nearly bumped into my grandfather. He looked exactly like the last time I saw him. His beige wrinkle-free London Fog raincoat covered his dark suit. Shuffling the brim of his white Stetson through his hands, he gently smiled. Then he set his hat on the coffee table, and gave us a big hug.

Nobody ever told me, but I always knew my grandfather was a powerful man. Even when Father was alive, I knew Grandfather was more important than him. Grandfather's presence made Father act different. Father's voice softened and he didn't yell. The guns disappeared and so did the vodka. They didn't seem to like each other, because when Grandfather visited, he sat with my father in our living room for hours, without speaking. In fact, they sat there all day without even looking at one another.

Somehow I knew Grandfather's appearance meant Mrs. Lane would never come back. Somehow, I knew Mother had made a bad decision in trusting her. But I also knew my grandfather would not be so naïve.

The day of Father's funeral, we got up early, and Mrs. Joseph helped us get dressed. I took a bath and she poured conditioner on my hair and combed out all the tangles. I put on my new blue dress and sat in the living room, waiting for Sheila and Nora. James and Brian came out of the bedroom in their new dark suits. Brian's hair didn't stick up as usual. James looked intelligent and mature, more like a grownup than a kid.

From the picture window, I saw Grandfather's car pull into the cul-de-sac in front of the house. Al stepped out of the passenger side, dressed in a dark blue suit. He looked much older than the last time I saw him at the detention center. At sixteen, he stood eye to eye with Grandfather. The contacts that replaced his thick horned-rimmed glasses made his face look bare.

He walked into the living room with his shoulders back, tightening his tie. Nora and Brian ran up to him and began tugging on his arms for attention. Sheila immediately gave him a hug. I stood behind them, unsure of Al because he acted more like an adult then one of us kids. After the initial excitement died down, Al turned to me and gave me an uncomfortable hug.

Al followed Grandfather into the kitchen with Mrs. Joseph. I sat back down on the sofa and stared out the window into the cul-de-sac. A long black shiny limousine pulled to the curb and our neighbor, Mrs. Rouse, stepped out.

Grandfather gathered us together and helped all of us, except Al, pile into the limousine. Al shoved his hands deep into his pockets and followed Grandfather to his car. I wanted to stick my head out the window and remind Al that he was still a kid just like the rest of us.

Inside the limo, I sat across from Mrs. Rouse. Her long legs stretched out in the wide-open space between us. Her folded fingers rested gently on top of the small black patent leather purse in her lap. Her short brown hair curled in neat little puffs all over her head. Bright red lipstick outlined her full lips.

Without staring at her, I tried to figure out what she was thinking. With her sad brown eyes, she silently watched us. Searching my brain, I tried to think of something funny. Anything that would make her sadness go away. I knew her sadness had to do with my father. That his death had affected them too. After all, we shared the same wall, the same front porch, and the same sidewalk. I knew they'd heard the gunshots. If only I could think of something to make it all go away.

To take my mind off the funeral, I stared at the electric windows. Everything in me wanted to push the buttons and watch the glass go up and down. I wanted to move around and try all the seats, to sit next to Mrs. Rouse and ride backwards. There were so many things to explore; I hoped the ride took a long time.

The car slowed as it went over a big dip in the road at the cemetery's open iron gates. Inside the entrance, old gravestones in different shapes and sizes dotted the grass. I imagined the bones of all those dead people lying in their boxes, all facing the sky. I imagined Father's dead body, still with skin and hair, lying in his coffin, facing the sky. I wondered if he was wearing those ugly brown boots.

We drove around a circle and the car stopped at the bottom of a little hill. The driver came around and opened the door, and I stepped onto the grass. At the very top of the hill, under an awning, Father's flag-draped coffin sat on a stand in front of a few rows of folding chairs.

People were gathered in small groups all over the hill. Some I recognized, others were strangers. Mother's good friend, Mrs. Haithcock, leaned against a big tree. I thought about the sweater she once knitted for Mother in exchange for a needlepoint chair cover. Mother's boss, Mr. Fowler, stood with some other people I recognized from Mother's office.

Of the other faces, some I knew, but didn't know their names. I couldn't remember if they were friends of Father's or Mother's. They stood in their little groups, talking and nodding. But when we started up the hill, it seemed a spirit waved over the crowd and made everyone stop. Even the birds stopped chirping.

On the grass, to the right of the coffin, stood Mrs. Lane. She looked exactly the same, with that odd braid neatly in place. I scrunched up my nose and stared at her, hoping she'd just disappear.

I thought we'd never get to the top of the hill. The piercing eyes of all those people made the air feel thick. It was like we were on a stage, doing a performance, mesmerizing the crowd without having to say a word.

When we made it to the top under the awning, the spirit broke and the spectators went back to their conversations. A nice man in a dark suit told us to sit in the front row. "The first seat is for your mother," he said kindly. "Then sit oldest down to the youngest."

I looked at the chairs and mentally counted down the line. Mother, Al, James, Sheila ... me. I sat in my chair. Sheila sat on my left and Brian on my right. Mrs. Rouse helped Nora onto her chair at the end of the row.

The flag over the coffin aggravated me. It seemed too respectable and too honorable for my father. Something in me wanted to jump up, slide it over, and lift up the lid. I wanted proof his body was really in that box. I wanted to see if he wore those brown suede boots.

Afraid the impulse would overtake me and I'd jump up and do something crazy, I overly concentrated on my feet. How short they were and how they didn't reach the ground. Everything happening around me felt so big compared to how small I was. The people gathered on the hill seemed to know more about what happened than me. If only I was bigger, I thought, it would all make more sense.

Maybe, if I turned around and looked hard at all the people, I could stare them down until they looked away. But I caught Grandfather's gaze instead. I didn't realize he had quietly sat down behind me. Not wanting to make him angry, I tucked my hands under my thighs and swung my feet back and forth, hoping my energy would fly through my toes.

I'll never understand how I knew Mother's car had arrived, but I sensed she was there. Nobody said, "Hey, Ellen, your mother's here." Or, "Ellen, honey, here comes your mother." Maybe I saw everyone stop and stare, I'm not sure. But when I turned around, I knew she was in the blue car that pulled up behind our limo.

Two men in dark blue suits got out and one of them opened the back door. Mother's foot stepped on the grass, and her face appeared above the car door. She wrapped her hands through the arms of both men, and with her head down and her steps heavy, she climbed the grassy hill. Tears poured out from her puffy eyes and ran in two steady streams down her face.

I wanted to get up and slide into her seat so she would have to sit in the middle of us. Why did she only have Al seated next to her? Why didn't that man put her seat right in the middle of ours? She should have sat between Sheila and me. After all, Al couldn't possibly love her the way we did. He couldn't comfort her as much as Sheila and me. I couldn't believe nobody was seated on her left.

With tears still trickling down her cheeks, Mother took her seat without even looking down the line at us. The weight of her sadness tightened the knot in my chest. Sucking in deep breaths through my nose, I tried to think of anything besides my Father and Mother. But no matter what I did, Mother's sadness pressed hard and heavy against me.

Mother never stopped crying. The preacher read softly from a small black book. Her sniffles rose above his deep gentle voice. As he spoke, sailors dressed in Navy uniforms with Popeye hats lined up along the road. They stood at attention, with the butts of their guns resting on the ground. I kept my eyes open and stared at the coffin as the preacher said a prayer. After the "amens," the sailors lifted their rifles toward the sky.

The shots echoed across the cemetery. *Kaboom!* Then they cocked their guns. *Kaboom!* Then the click-click of the reload. *Kaboom!* Nobody moved. A few crickets scraped their legs. Then, off in the distance, a lone bugler played "Taps." I sang along in my head, "Day is done, gone the sun ..."

More soldiers, wearing different uniforms, marched around the coffin and picked up the edges of the flag. Their hands, in immaculate white gloves, folded it like the triangular footballs I made out of paper. One of them took the football-shaped flag and stood at attention in front of Mother. With a stiff back, he bent over and spoke softly as he handed her the flag. Then they all marched off toward a white bus. Their duty for the day done. How odd, they were so serious and they didn't even know my father. If they had known him, would they have bothered to show respect?

Mother, still crying, turned to Al like the rest of us were not even there, and handed him the flag. She didn't walk down the line and give us each a hug or even say goodbye. She just stood up, and the two men in suits walked over and took their place by her side. The crowd didn't move as the trio walked back down the hill. The slam of doors echoed and the engine started. The car backed away from the limo and made its way around the circle and out the gate.

People in the chairs stood up, but I stayed in my seat, shocked over how much Mother didn't act like herself. It had to be because all those other people were there. Their presence made Mother act so strange. Besides, the two men wouldn't let her go. If all those people had stayed home, Mother would have acted differently. She would have only paid attention to her children. We would have all gathered around and buried Father together. All of us could have shared our pain without anyone watching.

Grandfather and Mrs. Rouse quickly ushered us back to the car. None of the gawkers started to leave until our doors shut. They were filing off the hill when we turned through the gate. All those nosy people who came for a show, just like the neighbors across the street the day Father died.

The limo turned down Buchanan Street and pulled up in front of our house. For the first time since the shooting, I went back inside. Grandfather told us to get changed, so I ran up the stairs. The strong smell of cleanser filled my nose. It never dawned on me someone had to clean up the mess. Sop up my father's blood, empty it into a bucket and throw the water out. Did they use the strong cleanser to try and erase the presence of my father's death from the house? If so, it didn't work.

Immediately, I ran into the boys' room. There, in the middle of the floor, was a dark round stain. Some of Father's blood had seeped deep into the wood. My mind made an instant association with that scent and my father's death. For years, I'd be somewhere—a mall, hospital, or a friend's house—and I'd smell it again. I'd recognize it instantly. Out of the blue, my mind would snap back to Father's body, and back to the first day I saw the stain.

Without mentioning a word about the stain or the shooting, we moved back into our now clean house. Grandfather slept in Mother's room without the door. A few days later, Grandmother arrived and took over the house. She made us clean our rooms and help her fix dinner. But she seemed far away, like her body was with us, but not her brain. She seemed sad, but I never saw her cry.

James and Brian, ignoring the stain, went back to life in their room. Sheila, Nora, and I again stretched out across the small space of our room.

The day after the funeral we went back to school. The other kids didn't seem to know what to say. At first they didn't talk to me. Then they began to ask what happened. One by one, they kept bugging me to tell them the story. Their eyes were wide with curiosity.

I felt powerful for having the story of the day. The attention filled a deep void in my soul. I told them to wait until recess. All day, the kids stared at me. When the bell rang, we piled onto the field behind Claremont Elementary. I told the four or five kids around me to wait. I'd tell them one at a time. I took the first girl and we walked to the edge of the soccer field. I tried to explain how mean Father was, how he had guns and beat my mother. How he tried to kill her but she fired first. How she was ready for him when he beat down the door.

Back in the classroom, while the other kids talked in little groups, I sat all alone at my desk. They kept turning and staring at me. I knew what they were doing, that they were comparing notes. The kids I told were telling the kids I hadn't. Their whispering gossip shushed around the room; my face burned in the fury of their words.

Then one of the kids from Buchanan Street shouted from across the room, "Ellen was in her backyard laughing on the day her father died."

Something inside me snapped. I thought I had explained everything so well. I thought the other kids understood. I traced over my story, thinking I'd made it so clear. Maybe I forgot to say the policeman told us to go in the backyard and not think about what happened. I was laughing, playing with Brian's cars.

I was trying not to think about my mother, the police, and my father's body.

Then, the knot in my chest went nuts. It came up into my throat and odd sounding sobs came out of my mouth. For the first time since the shooting, I cried. Once I started, I couldn't stop. My sobs turned into shuddering hiccups. I trembled as a flood of tears broke free.

In an instant, Miss Booker's arm came around my shoulder. She ordered the kids to get away and sit in their seats. She scooped me up and carried me to the chair next to her desk, sat down and wrapped her arms around me and rocked back and forth. I buried my face into her chest, trying to think of something else, trying to mentally make the other kids go away.

Suddenly, my knot began to unravel. Afraid of where it might lead, the adult inside my head began coaching the crying child. Whispering, telling her to think about something else. To push the mocking children far out of her mind. I wanted to run, but had nowhere to go. I tried to find something else to think about, but couldn't. Finally, trying to think about something else became the distraction I needed to stop crying.

I spent the rest of the day alone at my desk, deeply troubled. Nothing had turned out the way I thought it would. Then a new fear crept in. If I told people the truth and they distorted the facts, how could I ever be a normal kid? If they were going to form conclusions without all the information, what could I do?

That afternoon, I ran all the way home. I sat on the front porch and waited for James. He was the only person who could help me make sense of it all. As soon as I saw him coming down the sidewalk, I ran to meet him. Not sure how to begin, I blurted it all out. Barely coming up for air I told him how the kids got it all wrong. Patiently, James let me get all the way to the end of my story.

We stopped on the front porch and he turned to me. His eyes were gentle and filled with my pain. "Ellen, you don't have to tell anyone about Father's death. I don't tell my friends."

What a relief.

It would be four years before I told anyone else how my father died. After Mother moved us away from Arlington, I decided to never tell anyone about his death. But a friend let curiosity get the best of her. She begged me until I broke down and told her what happened. I carefully stressed the details of Father's abuse. The knot came back as I expressly said how he had it coming. I didn't tell her about the laughter.

A giddy excitement filled her eyes as I revealed my secret. The fear still buried inside my chest made my teeth rattle. I clenched my jaw together to push the fear back down. I folded my fingers together to control my shakes. I begged her not to tell anyone, even her family. But she didn't keep her promise.

About a year later, I dated her brother. He too became curious about my father's death. Feeling more comfortable, I told him my secret. Once again, my teeth chattered when the fear came back up. When I finished, he said, "I already knew. I just wanted to hear it from you."

My heart dropped to the floor. First because I'd been betrayed, and then because my secret was out. I couldn't stop thinking about who else knew. And wondering how my friend explained it and how much she distorted the truth.

That day I had a new gawker in the people who had heard the gossip. Only, unlike the day of Father's funeral, the new ones could be anywhere. I had no way of knowing who they were or what they knew. I started worrying that day. Worrying about what people thought of my mother and what they thought about all of us.

AUNT JEANNE MARIE

IN MOTHER'S ABSENCE, LOTS OF PEOPLE I had never met regularly came by our house. Most of them brought meals and, normally, Grandmother told us when they were coming. But not a word was said about the beautiful woman in our living room. Something didn't seem right when, just before lunch, I came charging through the front door and found her seated in the folding chair beside Father's desk. By her fair skin and sandy blond hair, I sensed we might be related. Or maybe I recognized her from the steady stream of photos that came in the mail. But why didn't Grandmother tell us company was coming?

But there she sat, upright in the chair, with both feet planted flat on the floor. Her hair was curled close to her head, and she had short bangs parted down the middle that flipped slightly upwards on both sides of her forehead. She looked proper, like a teacher, with her white cotton blouse buttoned to the top and her dark blue skirt spread neatly across her lap. Delicately, she balanced a saucer on her knees, while both of her hands caressed the cup close to her lips, as if it could warm her whole body.

When I stopped just inside the front door, the china softly clinked as she set the cup down on the saucer. She looked me in the eye and in a warm voice, with just a hint of excitement said, "Hello, Ellen." I got the feeling she'd been waiting all morning for me to come see her.

Surprised she knew my name, I walked over to her. She put her arm around my waist and drew me in close and gave me a gentle hug. "I'm your Aunt Jeanne Marie. Your mother's sister."

At my age, "sisters" were all little girls. I couldn't imagine grown women as sisters, even though I knew Mother had two.

Besides, I had no idea what grown sisters were like, because I'd never met any of my aunts.

I did know a little about Aunt Jeanne Marie. When Mother talked about her, she sounded so exotic. She and my Uncle Eugene were missionaries somewhere in a foreign country. She had written Mother many times from different places all over the world. Her life sounded exciting and I had always wanted to meet her. And now she sat in our living room, right in front of me.

Aunt Jeanne Marie seemed interested in getting to know me, but I knew if Grandmother found me, she'd send me right back outside without a drink of water. Quickly, I said an awkward "hello," and slipped out of her hug. Bolting through the swinging door to the kitchen, I leaned over the sink and filled a cup from the tap. Then I walked back to the doorway and stared at Aunt Jeanne Marie while I drank the whole glass down.

Everything about her looked too beautiful for our worn-out living room. The graceful way she sat made her look out of place beside the papers that cluttered the top of Father's desk. Her eyes danced and the corners of her lips turned slightly upward like she was about to smile. Nothing about her seemed stressed or worn out like all the other adults.

Leaving my empty glass in the sink, I left the kitchen and Aunt Jeanne Marie watched me walk across the living room and out the front door. I joined the kickball game in front of our house, but for the first time I really didn't want to play. I wanted to go back inside and watch my aunt.

When Grandmother called me in for lunch, I didn't hesitate. Aunt Jeanne Marie was already at the table when I plopped down on the bench across from her with a large platter of peanut butter and jelly sandwiches between us. Up on my knees, I reached for a sandwich, but she told me to wait. The room filled with chatter as my brothers and sisters all sat down. One by one they too reached for sandwiches, but she told them the same thing.

After we all sat down she said, "Don't forget to say grace."

I didn't want to close my eyes or put my head down. So I squinted to allow myself to see around the table. When all my brothers and sisters heads were bowed, Aunt Jeanne Marie closed her eyes and bowed hers.

She spoke slowly and precisely. "Let the words of my mouth and the meditations of my heart be acceptable to you, Oh Lord, my God and my Redeemer. Amen."

Thankfully, the prayer was short, but I didn't understand why we said it. Especially since it had nothing to do with food. Good thing she said "amen," or I'd still be sitting there with my head down.

All through lunch, Aunt Jeanne Marie eagerly listened to everything we said. When we said something funny, she tilted her head back and laughed out loud as if we were the funniest kids in the world. When we spoke, she looked us in the eye, nodding her head to let us know she understood. I kept waiting for her to get frustrated with our constant chattering and fidgeting, but she never did.

After the sandwiches were gone, Grandfather put a platter of vanilla wafers on the table, and my siblings and I were up on our elbows grabbing as many as we could. Expecting Aunt Jeanne Marie to tell us to "settle down" or "be quiet," I watched her out of the corner of my eye. But she never said a negative word to any of us.

The day after Aunt Jeanne Marie arrived, Grandmother and Grandfather packed their things and left. Grandfather checked into a hotel off Columbia Pike and Grandmother went home to Texas. Grandfather said she needed rest, but I knew she was mad. I learned later, Grandmother had told Aunt Jeanne Marie to stay home, but she disobeyed and came anyway.

But I was glad. Things were better with Aunt Jeanne Marie. Instead of fussing at us over chores, she made a list and taped it to the refrigerator under a sign she made that said, "Confucius Says: No Workee, No Eatee."

One night while on kitchen duty with Aunt Jeanne Marie, I dried the dishes while she washed. After the last dish went in the cabinets, I threw my towel on the counter and headed for the door. But her soft voice stopped me.

"Ellen, honey, what about sweeping the floor?"

Letting out a deep sigh, I picked up the broom and quickly swept the floor, ignoring the corners and under the dining room table. Before I shoved the broom between the refrigerator and the wall, her voice stopped me again. "Ellen, honey. Don't forget the corners." She hadn't even looked up from wiping off the counters. How did she know I missed the corners?

Taking my time, I again swept over the entire floor. I emptied the dustpan and put away the broom. I headed for the door, but her voice stopped me again. "Thank you, Ellen. You did such a wonderful job helping me clean the kitchen, especially with the floor."

"You're welcome," I said, as the door flapped behind me. But why did she compliment me? Didn't she realize I only did a good job because she made me? Without her coaxing, I wouldn't have done it at all. I shook my head and wandered into the living room. Did Aunt Jeanne Marie not see the real me? She treated me as though I decided, by myself, to clean the kitchen floor. As if I did it right the first time.

It didn't take long for Aunt Jeanne Marie to become a mystery I needed to solve. So I began to watch everything she did.

One afternoon, I found her at the dining room table with an assortment of colored markers spread out. When she saw me, she slid over on the bench and I sat down next to her.

"What are you doing?" I asked.

"I'll show you." She picked up the piece of paper and held it in front of me. In different colors on every other line she'd written, "I Love You."

Her eyes brightened and she smiled. "It's for your uncle," she said. "I want him to know how much I love him."

Jealously panged in my heart. Having never met Uncle Eugene, he didn't seem real to me. Aunt Jeanne Marie wrote him every day, and she talked about him constantly, but I didn't want her to love him that much. I was afraid if she did, there wouldn't be enough left for us. But she cared a lot about him, so I tried to care about him too.

"Where is Uncle Eugene?" I asked, not really wanting to know the answer.

"He's at our home in Bogotá, Columbia. Do you know where that is, Ellen?"

I shook my head no.

"It's in South America. We have an apartment there near the airport. The planes fly in so close I can see their bellies. We're on the top floor, with a sweeping view of the Andes Mountains. Maybe some day you'll go there. It's a beautiful place."

"Do you miss it?" I asked, hoping the answer was no.

"I miss the people. I love them very much. But if I was there, I couldn't be here with you guys. And I would rather be here with you."

Aunt Jeanne Marie set her paper back down and picked up a red marker and wrote another line of "I love you." It seemed silly to me that a grown woman would write a note to a grown man in the same way I wrote one to my mother. I never knew grownups did things like that. I wondered what my uncle was like and why my aunt loved him so much. I hoped he was as wonderful as her.

It didn't take long for a routine to develop around the house. Every couple days, Grandfather came by, but mostly he stayed busy with Mother's case. Aunt Jeanne Marie worked so hard that every afternoon she closed herself in our room and took a nap.

One Saturday, a homemade "Do Not Disturb" sign hung from her doorknob with a picture of a serious tiger standing guard. Next to him was written, "Leave that Aunt Alone!"

The hour separation was impossible for me to bear. Ignoring the sign, I snuck in the room and crawled onto the bed next to her. To put her mind at ease, I said, "Don't worry, I'm here to protect you from the other kids. I won't let any of them come in."

Aunt Jeanne Marie laughed and put her arm over her eyes and fell asleep. I lay still next to her, my chest calm, my heart softened. Never had I felt so relaxed. I listened to every breath she took in and every one she let out. I hoped she never went away.

It didn't take me long to learn God was really important to her. One slip of "Oh my God," brought her firmest correction. "Ellen, honey, He means so much to me; even 'gosh' is too close."

In the mornings, as we headed off to school, Aunt Jeanne Marie held open the screen door and said, "Goodbye, darlings. Have a good day." In the afternoons, instead of dreading going home, I looked forward to seeing her at the front door. Her cheery voice greeted us with, "Hello, sugars. How was your day?" Then she helped us unload our books and lunch boxes.

Every night after her bath, she changed into her nightgown and robe and stood at the bathroom sink, covering her face with a thin layer of white Ponds cold cream. After a few seconds massaging it in, she wiped it off with a damp washcloth.

One night, finding her alone in the bathroom, I sat on the closed toilet lid and watched as the crisp scent of the cream filled the room. I just wanted to hear her gentle voice so I started asking questions.

"What are you doing?"

"Taking care of my skin."

I tucked my knees into my chest, wrapped my arms tight around my legs, and gently rocked. Soaking up her presence, afraid the conversation would stop, like a three–year-old I blurted out, "Why?"

She didn't miss a beat, "Because the more you do for your skin, the kinder it will be to you later."

I needed more questions, but I couldn't think of any. I just wanted to keep her talking.

"Why do you use that stuff?"

"It makes my skin soft."

"Why do you need soft skin?"

"Because your uncle likes it that way."

It was almost bedtime, so I ran from the bathroom and climbed the ladder of our triple bunk beds and waited for Aunt Jeanne Marie to tuck me in. The overhead light was still on when my sisters climbed into their beds. As I pulled the covers over me, I smelled my aunt's cold cream.

She climbed the first couple rungs and leaned in and kissed my cheek. She was right; the skin on her face was irresistibly soft. She went to the middle bunk and kissed Sheila, and I leaned my head over as she bent into the bottom bunk and kissed Nora good night.

Then she touched the foot of each bed and said, "God, put angels on their bedposts."

Lying on my stomach, I rested my chin in the palms of my hands. Aunt Jeanne Marie shut off the light then turned in the doorway and said goodnight. Long streams from the hall light fell around her. The raglan sleeves of her robe flowed when she lifted her arms, making her look angelic. I wanted the moment to last so I stopped her with more questions. I don't remember what I asked and I didn't care what the answers were. I just wanted the moment to linger.

Overcome with emotion, my mind searched for something to say about the way I felt. I didn't want her to go away without knowing I saw what she did for us. How she loved us, even when we didn't deserve it.

Finally I blurted out, "I got it Aunt Jeanne Marie. You're our fairy godmother."

She laughed softly. "Good night, darlings." Then she turned off the hall light and I listened to her gentle footsteps fade away as she walked down the stairs.

In the dark, I rolled over on my back and tucked my hands underneath my head. I stretched out my legs and crossed my ankles and looked up at the ceiling. The streetlight pouring through the open curtains turned the room black and white.

Yeah, that's it. She's our fairy godmother. Just for me and my brothers and sisters.

I didn't believe there were angels on my bedpost. But Aunt Jeanne Marie was real. She was here and she belonged to us. I didn't have to wonder if she loved me. I just knew she did. I didn't have to wonder if she'd take care of us. I just knew she would.

Staring at the ceiling, I was proud of myself for telling her how I felt. For the first time, I felt safe in my room with my sisters. I could feel something out there guiding me. Something really big that sent my aunt to take care of us. And for the first time in my life, I felt hope.

MOTION FOR INQUIRY DE LUNATICO

WHILE THE JOSEPHS WERE TAKING CARE of us bewildered Gibson kids, a war began to rage between the factions who loved my mother ... and Mrs. Lane, my father's strongest supporter.

If the news of Father's death outraged Mrs. Lane, she hid it well on the morning of the shooting when Mother called her from the house. As the only lawyer my mother knew, and one she thought of as a personal friend, Mrs. Lane seemed the best choice to defend her. That morning, Mrs. Lane advised Mother to remain silent until she met with her at the jail.

So Mother clammed up, refusing any explanation for the shooting. And without any details, the police had no other choice but to charge her with murder. Mrs. Lane arrived at the jail in time to witness Mother being photographed and fingerprinted.

Once they were alone, Mother meticulously detailed the events of the past several days. She explained how Father pushed her into a desperate situation. How she feared he'd shoot her, then the five of us. She told Mrs. Lane about the night he drunkenly thought we had an intruder. How, in the dark, he shot his Luger in the living room. How the bullet holes were still in the doorjamb. How one ripped through the binding of our thick Fannie Farmer Cookbook. How the police came and did nothing.

Mother also told her all about Father's repeated ambushes during their separation. On that first morning, Mrs. Lane showed great compassion to Mother, without revealing any partiality toward Father.

Right after their first meeting, Mrs. Lane drove over to 1202 S. Buchanan Street. The house had not been touched since the shooting and the pool of blood in the boys' bedroom had dried. She gathered up some clothes for Mother, stopped by the Joseph's to console us then headed back to the jail.

By then, Mother had a list of everybody to call. Everyone, that is, except her parents. With their power and influence, she feared, even if the charges were dropped, they'd try to take custody of us kids. Or worse yet, split us up between them and her sister Elizabeth. She thought it better to wait until everything got settled before telling them the news. Besides, the last thing she wanted to hear was, "I told you so."

To Mother, the shooting seemed a clear case of self-defense. Foolishly, she thought it would be settled in a matter of days. She knew of Mrs. Lane's inexperience as a defense attorney, but the case just didn't seem that complicated. What with the pre-existing court records and eye witnesses to Father's abuse. Mother thought Mrs. Lane could easily handle it all.

What she never counted on was Mrs. Lane's devotion to my father.

While Mother was being booked at the Arlington County Jail, and after the ambulance and all the neighbors left, my uncle and his family pulled up to our vacant house. Excited about their visit, Uncle Fred and Aunt Peg had driven straight through from Delaware.

When Uncle Fred swung open the door and stepped out of his station wagon, he sensed something odd. He said for a warm Sunday afternoon, the entire neighborhood seemed too quiet.

Uncle Fred hummed as he headed up our walkway, followed by Aunt Peg and their four children. Years later, he told me how unusual it seemed that all the windows were shut and not a single sound seeped out from behind our closed door. He skipped the steps up to our porch, opened the screen and knocked.

Our neighbor's door opened and Mr. Rouse poked his head around his screen door. "Can I help you with something?" he asked.

"Yes … ah yes sir, I'm Fred Gibson," my uncle said in his

boisterous New England accent. "I've come to visit my brother, Ed, and his wife, Josephine. Have you seen them?"

Uncle Fred said all the blood ran out of Mr. Rouse's face. Looking dumbfounded, Mr. Rouse shook his head, "You ... you don't know what happened, do you?"

"Ah, no, what's wrong?"

Staring at Aunt Peg and the kids, Mr. Rouse hesitated. Uncle Fred turned to his wife and said, "Peg, I think you need to take the kids to the car."

Mr. Rouse stepped onto his porch and let the screen door slam behind him. Reaching over the rail he shook my uncle's hand. "I'm Herbert Rouse and I'm really sorry to have to tell you this."

Uncle Fred fumbled for the pack of cigarettes in his shirt pocket. Mr. Rouse's voice shook as he spoke. "Josephine shot Ed this morning. The police arrested her and she's down at the jail."

"Jeeesus Christ!" Uncle Fred said as smoke shot out his mouth and nostrils. "I feared something like this might happen."

Mr. Rouse let out a deep sigh, "Then you know some of the history."

"Yes, yes. And I'm just sick about it. Josephine is such a wonderful lady. And I love my brother dearly, but she's clearly not the perpetrator here."

Uncle Fred paced the small distance on our porch. Fidgeting, he lit another cigarette. Fearing Mother would be charged unfairly, he was anxious to get over to the jail to talk to the police.

Shaking his head in disbelief, Uncle Fred shook Mr. Rouse's hand again. "Thank you for breaking the news to me. I'm so sorry this has affected you and your family. I'm sure I'll see you again."

From our house, Uncle Fred dropped Peg and the kids off at their hotel. Then he made his way through heavy traffic to the police station. Standing at a short counter, he asked to speak with the person in charge of the Gibson case. After several minutes a plain-clothed officer came up and introduced himself as Detective Keyes.

Feeling nervous for Mother, Uncle Fred felt the pressing need to share his concerns. He leaned in close to the detective and said, "Look here sir, Edmund was my brother and I loved him, but he was a deeply troubled man. I can assure you, this woman is the victim, not the perpetrator."

"I understand, sir," Detective Keyes said, backing away from my uncle. "But we must do our job and look at every possible angle."

Undaunted, Uncle Fred's voice became stronger. "Let me make myself clear. Josephine is innocent, and I want you to know I'm willing to do whatever is necessary in her defense."

Detective Keyes nodded and spoke as if reading a prepared statement. "I understand, Mr. Gibson. And I can assure you, we will take everything into consideration."

As the detective turned to walk away, Mrs. Lane came up to the counter.

Detective Keyes recognized her and said, "Mrs. Lane, this is Mr. Gibson's brother, Fred."

"Hello Fred," she smiled. "I've heard a great deal about you from Edmund. He and Josephine are dear friends of mine …" Then she paused, "Oh, I'm sorry. Edmund *was* a dear friend of mine."

Surprised to know nothing about her, Uncle Fred stuck out his hand.

Mrs. Lane started describing to my uncle some of the technical details of Mother's case. The more she said, the more surprised my uncle became by her omission of Father's abuse. Finally, Uncle Fred stopped her and said, "Look here Helen, I knew my brother very well. I loved him, but he was a drunk and he abused Josephine. In no way is she at fault here. Josephine is a lovely woman, and she does not deserve to be charged with killing my brother."

Mrs. Lane became agitated, "Mr. Gibson, I can assure you

I'm doing everything possible to get Jo out of jail." Then she cut their conversation short. "As things progress, I'll keep you up to date."

Back in his hotel room, Uncle Fred began calling family, beginning with his and Father's sister, Lenore. Lenore became enraged over the shooting. She didn't like the way Uncle Fred defended Mother, even though she and Father had never been close. After a heated conversation, Lenore insisted on calling Mrs. Lane herself.

After Mrs. Lane's meeting with my uncle, she went back to the jail. According to her timesheet, during her visit with Mother, she received the call from Aunt Lenore. The two strong women butted heads. An argument ensued, and Mrs. Lane noted on her timesheet: "Phone call from Mrs. Kirwin, deceased's sister from Baltimore, while in jail with Jo. Threatened to come down immediately, etc."

Two days after the shooting, Mother entered Judge Dodge's courtroom and stood next to Mrs. Lane at the defense table. Per Mrs. Lane's advice, Mother continued to remain silent, refusing to provide any explanation for the shooting. The Commonwealth's Attorney, fearing a *not guilty by temporary insanity* plea, moved for a chapter 19.1-228, or a *motion for an inquiry de lunatico*. The judge agreed and ordered Mother committed to a state mental hospital for pre-trial observation and a diagnosis as to her mental capacity to stand trial.

As the case became more complicated, Mrs. Lane called on Philip Hirschkop for assistance. Mr. Hirschkop, a young, inexperienced lawyer, had recently made a name for himself in *Loving vs. Virginia*. The national case made headlines for abolishing all race-based legal restrictions on marriage within the United States.

After speaking with Hirschkop, Mrs. Lane made a call to the Josephs and told James not to worry, but that Mother would not be getting out on bond.

A couple days later, according to her timesheet, Mrs. Lane

made another visit to Buchanan Street "… to meet detectives Keyes, Spedden; first on murder scene, Short and Coddle … Mr. Coddle remembered prior episode of shooting wildly into bookcases and ceiling."

By the end of the first week, Mother started to get uncomfortable about the direction of the case. When Mrs. Lane ignored Mother's repeated insistence that our long-time family physician be contacted for the evidence he had of Father's abuse, Mother got mad. When Mrs. Lane finally did call the doctor, Mother still had to prod her to motion the court for a detailed interview with him prior to the decision on the *motion for an inquiry de lunatico*.

In the mean time, a long line of witnesses started coming forward in defense of my mother. Blanche de Clercq, one of Mother's oldest friends, called Mrs. Lane personally and gave detailed descriptions of Father's abuse. Our old neighbor, Mr. Uhler wrote an unsolicited letter to the judge, offering to fill out an affidavit to prior episodes of Father's violence. One neighbor across the street spent an entire day sitting outside the judge's office, waiting to tell him about Father's treatment of Mother. It turned out, on the night Father held Mother at gunpoint at the dining room table, he saw it all through our picture window. He had made the call that brought the police to our doorstep.

But nowhere, according to Mrs. Lane's five-page time sheet, did she spend any time investigating Father's violence. In fact, she waited eight days before meeting with the Rouses. The people who shared our walkway and front porch, the same people who heard the shots through our shared wall.

Several days later, without saying anything to Mother, Mrs. Lane picked James and Sheila up from the Joseph's and drove them to Mr. Hirschkop's office. Leaving Sheila alone in a large empty waiting room, she ushered James into a small room for a taped interview. Afterwards, without James or any other adults present, she brought Sheila in and questioned her about the shooting.

Still in shock, less than a week after the shooting, Mother signed over a blanket Power of Attorney to Mrs. Lane that covered all her affairs, including anything pertaining to us children. "Of course," Mrs. Lane had said, "it can be revoked any time you desire, or when you get out."

Then Mrs. Lane, Aunt Lenore and Uncle Fred, made all Father's funeral arrangements.

After their initial conversation, Aunt Lenore and Mrs. Lane became friends. Mrs. Lane, using her Power of Attorney, sent Aunt Lenore over to the Navy Yard to pick up Father's personal belongings. Since Father never kept any of his important papers at home, his file box contained all the papers needed to get benefits flowing for Mother.

Uncle Fred, who suffered from his own alcohol problems, began to drink heavily. He and Lenore fought bitterly over issues Uncle Fred later refused to share with me. Two days before Father's funeral, Lenore, in a rage, packed up all her stuff, including Father's papers, and went home to Baltimore.

That same day, Mrs. Lane picked Al up at the train station in Alexandria and took him back to her office for a lengthy untaped interview. She noted on her timesheet: "Alfred ... completely at ease, showed great depth of understanding and affection for both parents." By the time she brought him over to see us at the Joseph's, we weren't home.

Based on her timesheet, for the first week of Mother's incarceration, Mrs. Lane spent all her time trying to justify Father's mental demise. Her focus turned away from Mother's defense toward attempting to prove Father's violence resulted from stress at work. In a note to Uncle Fred she wrote;

> *Did Ed express in letters or directly to you any doubt about his ability to carry work loads given to him at the office? Had he been upped recently beyond his stam? I'm digging into the Workmen's Compensation rules and regulations ... Think hard! ... Did he express any grumpiness about the*

amount of work, or about a lack of office help? ... I've also asked Jo these questions as well as asking about the amount of work brought home. Grasping at every straw that imagination can grasp at."

Except, of course, at the big long straw pointing to my father's senseless abuse of my mother.

When Mother received the following letter from Mrs. Lane, she realized she'd lost control of her case.

Dear Jo,
Please put on your thinking cap and try to remember if there have been any indications in the past year or so of work pressure on Ed. Has he brought work home very often? If so, how often? Has it caused sleeplessness, etc? Has he (or as Phil reminds us, HAD) he been given extra responsibility a bit beyond him? Might this have caused the drinking, even at a time when he had expressed great joy at being taken back into the home situation? I need to know any indication of these things in order to consider the possibility of getting Workmen's Compensation.

As soon as you are back, I want to lend you one of my favorite books, The Courage to be Happy, *by Dorothy (wife of Sinclair Lewis). It has given me many lifts and inspiration at oddly variant times.*

Affectionately, Helen

That letter finally proved to Mother that Mrs. Lane had ulterior motives. She was convinced that getting her charges dropped was not her lawyer's primary goal.

When the police told Mother a decision must be made for the long-term care of us kids, Mother finally surrendered to the truth that she must fire Mrs. Lane. And in order to do that, she needed her parents.

My grandparents received her call at their home in Dallas while packing for a trip to Mt. Pleasant for my great-grandmother's funeral. Already grieving the loss of her own mother, my grandmother was devastated by the nightmare in Arlington, the image of her daughter sitting in jail, and her grandchildren in the home of strangers. The following day, my grandfather caught the first flight to Virginia, while Grandmother drove to East Texas to bury my great-grandmother.

As soon as he arrived, Grandfather retained the State of Virginia's most accomplished trial attorney, the renowned T. Brooke Howard. Leaving the termination of Lane and Herschkop to Mother, Grandfather didn't say anything to Mrs. Lane when she came by the house after Father's funeral. She and a private detective wanted to look for pictures of Father, James, and Sheila, for Mother's defense. Grandfather was polite but said nothing about her upcoming removal from the case.

Two weeks after the shooting, Grandfather met with Mrs. Lane at her office and requested a breakdown of all the hours she'd spent working on Mother's defense. He then visited Mother and told her to draft a letter to her prior lawyers asking them to petition the courts for removal from the case.

That same day, Mrs. Lane called my Grandfather and said she needed all the children at home on the following Wednesday to take pictures and show "position of actors both in past and recent events." Again, my grandfather was polite but distant, and did not mention her impending termination.

On Sunday, Grandmother arrived and immediately phoned Mrs. Lane. In a heated conversation, Grandmother demanded to know why she allowed Mother be taken to a mental hospital. Her knowledge of Mrs. Lane's impending removal didn't take the edge off her rage. Mrs. Lane added the thirty-minute conversation to my grandfather's bill.

That Wednesday, Mrs. Lane picked up a registered letter from Mother asking for both her and Philip Hirschkop to go before the court and take themselves off the case. "It didn't sound like the Jo I have known for so long," she wrote in a letter to my Aunt Lenore.

In spite of her termination, Mrs. Lane kept her appointment and showed up at our house, with a photographer in tow. For thirty minutes, she stood on our front porch and argued with my grandparents. But they refused to let her in.

Even though she'd been removed from the case, Mrs. Lane billed my grandfather for the argument noting, "… Mr. Rice still said nothing about being off the case. Detained us for over one half hour with explanations of illness, trouble, and persecution. They made it clear that we were to stop our efforts right then and there, but nothing about a substitute attorney."

That same day Mother received a disturbing letter from Mrs. Lane. She began by going over some minor civil details of the case. Something about Father having waived his right to a life insurance policy through the Navy Department. Then she went on to say,

> *The legal advisor agreed with me that we may be able to show that Ed was incompetent to waive the $13,000 insurance and is sending me copies of those papers. Here's hoping! He loved his family and must have bitterly regretted that waiver signing, of course.*
>
> *… Be of good cheer—keep your writer's mind open and observant. Who knows—a book or article may come out of this.*
>
> *One very small matter, are the growing seeds your project or the children's? It may be a down–to–earth letter topic, (pardon the pun) to write about them. And is that what you saved egg boxes for? When Ed once complained about them (your habit of saving junk and creating a fire hazard) I told him I saved them also for starting seedlings. Ah me! Such is life!*
>
> *Affectionately, Mrs. Lane*

To this day I wonder whom those affections were really for.

Mother didn't waste any time forwarding the letter to her new attorney. Mr. Howard wrote back, "I am enclosing the letter written to you … by Mrs. H. Lane; after reading it more carefully, particularly the portions you have marked with red ink, I agree that the good lady was not trying to do you any good at the hospital."

After three weeks, all Mother's psychiatric tests were completed, and a sheriff's car was sent to pick her up. After packing her things, she sat on the edge of her bed, anxious to move on with her life. The head nurse who supervised her treatment came in and put her arm around Mother "Well, Josephine, you are right as apples. There is nothing wrong with you."

A truth Mother suspected, but needed to hear.

Late in the afternoon on Thursday, May 4th, Grandfather got the news that Mother's bond hearing would be the following day. With the banks closed and no cash on hand, he phoned a friend in DC who agreed to open up his bank. Within a few hours, Grandfather held three certified checks for $5,000, made out to the Arlington County Court. Grandfather hoped Mother's bond would not exceed his funds.

The following day, Grandmother looked exquisite in her perfectly fitting grey suit. The collar of her white silk blouse peeked over the lapel of her jacket and a small shiny red cherry pin rested on her lapel. Her long brownish-grey hair was twisted into a neat motherly bun on the back of her head, without a single hairpin showing.

Grandfather looked important in his dark-brown suit and stiffly pressed white shirt. Every piece of their clothing had been specifically selected to reflect the loving home my mother grew up in.

Me, I soaked it all in. After a week at the Joseph's and three weeks of people coming and going, I was ready to get on with my new "normal" life. And I couldn't wait to see my mother. I wanted her to come home where she belonged. In my childish way, I thought once she arrived, everything would be all right. And her return would make the horror of Father's death all go away. I really did think my grandparents had the power to pull it all off. I had no idea it was an impossible task.

THE HOMECOMING

ONE EARLY SATURDAY MORNING, while Mother was still in the hospital, I sat alone on the curb across the street from our house thinking about how, in spite of the dark hole of Mother's absence, life seemed to be getting better. With Aunt Jeanne Marie, it did seem possible we could become a normal family. Maybe, rebuild our lives. Get past Father's death and start to fit in. But I had no idea how much Father's death had affected Mother.

With my legs stretched out, I examined the latest wounds on my knees. The big purple spots from my fall off James' skateboard looked like gravel imbedded inside my skin. The scab on my other knee dangled by a thread. Though it was still painful to touch, I couldn't stop picking at it and making it bleed. Holding my breath, I pressed the dried crust hard against the reopened wound, hoping it would reattach.

Squinting in the bright sun, I looked up at our house. The rows of forsythia bushes along the front were filled with bright yellow blooms. If Mother were home, she wouldn't waste any time cutting a big bundle and stuffing them into a vase on the dining room table. She'd smile as she spread them out in a wide bouquet. I took a deep breath, imagining their fresh vanilla scent filling the downstairs.

From the outside, nothing had changed since Father's death, except for the now empty flagpole. But inside, everything had. Dishes no longer piled in the sink. The laundry didn't collect in the kitchen. And the fresh clean smell of cleanser replaced the stale odor from Father's pipe.

Just then, Aunt Jeanne Marie came through the back gate, carrying a brown paper bag full of trash. The sun filtered through her blond hair, brightening it around her face like a light bulb.

Her full skirt swayed from side to side and her swinging arms brushed against their folds. When she walked, she raised slightly on the balls of her feet, causing a little bounce to her step. By the way her chin tilted from side to side, I could tell she was humming a song. At the base of the flagpole, she lifted the lid to the trashcan and dropped in the bag.

An image of Father standing in that same spot, his Confederate flag draped over his shoulder, flashed in my mind. I shivered and the hairs on my arms perked up. If he were alive, he'd be the one walking through the back gate. He'd be whistling a song while attaching the flag to the string. I'd be watching his stiff expression as the flag jerked up the pole.

Without seeing me, Aunt Jeanne Marie turned around, walked back through the side yard, and disappeared through the back gate. I stood up and went inside to see what she was doing.

The empty living room had gone through its daily transition from Aunt Jeanne Marie's bedroom. Her "bed" was folded up and her nightgown and robe put away. The neatly fluffed flowered pillows on the sleeping chair struggled to draw your eyes away from the wood popping through the holes in the arms. On the table by the chair, her white leather Bible sat underneath a small black book. The curtains were open, allowing the bright sunshine to flood the small room.

The running water in the kitchen shut off, and Aunt Jeanne Marie came through the swinging door. I knew this was the time she sat and read, but I wanted to be near her. When she saw me standing by the front door, a broad smile spread across her face, showing all of her bright white teeth. "Hello, honey, how ya doin?" The gentle words loosened the knot in my chest.

"Okay, I guess."

Aunt Jeanne Marie sat down in the sleeping chair, scooted over, and patted the cushion next to her. I plopped down and leaned up against her. All the muscles in my shoulders relaxed as I rested my head on her chest and listened to the faint sound of her heartbeat. The crisp smell of her freshly shampooed hair still lingered in the air.

There were so many questions about Aunt Jeanne Marie I still wanted answered but, with the five of us, I rarely caught her alone. Taking advantage of the moment, I began, "Aunt Jeanne Marie, why don't you have any kids of your own?"

She smiled and tightened her arm around my shoulder. "Well, I wanted them, but I could never seem to have any. But God gave me you guys instead, and I'm so glad he did."

My heart sank. It never dawned on me Aunt Jeanne Marie wanted kids of her own. I felt guilty for being glad she didn't have any. Even I knew if she did have kids, she wouldn't have come to stay with us. But why did God deprive her of kids only to give her us? How could she be glad about this arrangement?

The unfairness of life overwhelmed me. How could Aunt Jeanne Marie not be mad that Mother and Father had six kids and she didn't have any? Obviously, she and Uncle Eugene would have been good parents. Plus, how could she be excited about getting us instead of kids of her own? Didn't she realize we were a booby prize? How could she thank God for this? But God seemed so real to her. I needed more information, so I blurted out the most obvious question. "Aunt Jeanne Marie, how do you know there is a God?"

A gentle smile broke across her face and her chin slightly rose. Her eyes closed for a second while she digested my question. She opened them, placed her hands on my shoulders, and turned my body toward her.

"Imagine, Ellen, you don't know me. Imagine someone came to you, pointed at me and said, 'That woman over there loves you.' You'd shrug and say, 'Okay.' But you really wouldn't believe it, would you?"

Not sure what to say, I shook my head no.

Aunt Jeanne Marie closed her lips and quietly breathed in through her nose. She thought for a few more seconds, then her eyes lit up. She put her arms around me and gave me a tight hug, "But what if I came up to you, put my arms around you, and said, 'Ellen, honey, I love you.' You would believe me right?"

Not really sure if I would, I nodded yes anyway. But, the thought of some stranger loving me seemed ridiculous. Especially since I thought most people didn't like me. But Aunt Jeanne Marie was different. She didn't have to tell me she loved me, I just knew she did. But I didn't understand why.

"Sugar, one day, God will come to you and say, 'Ellen, I love you,' and you'll know it's Him."

Pretending to understand the depth of our conversation, I stared at the Bible. The pretty white cover with its gold zipper made me want one of my own. Not to read, just to have. Besides, I still couldn't understand why God had me born into this family. Why wasn't Aunt Jeanne Marie my mother? If He could do anything, why did I grow up the way I did? He could have made everything different. But He didn't.

After dinner, Grandfather came by the house to tell us Mother would be coming home soon. Up until that time, nobody had told me Mother went to jail. The adults told me about the hospital, and after seeing her at the funeral, I did think she needed to get well. But I didn't know there could still be a trial. That Mr. Howard had only arranged to post her bond. That Mother still faced a murder charge.

Grandfather sat on the sofa as the rest of us gathered around the dining room table to write Mother one last letter. Excited by the thought of her return, I used my best ten-year-old penmanship and wrote,

Dear Mother, Today I got my report card and I got 4 B's & 4 C's. Also, Miss Booker didn't have any comments. (I've been good Ha! Ha! That I doubt!)

Grandfather walked over to the table, smiled, and picked up a piece of paper. "I'll write her too," he said.

James wrote his letter in cursive. Brian, copying James, got up on his knees, bit his lip, and slowly wrote his letter in cursive too. Sheila pushed her long hair behind her shoulders and started to print in small letters. Trying to make mine fancy, I curved my t's and printed my letters clear and precise.

Not wanting to mention anything bad, I tried to think of funny things to say,

> *"... If my letter is wet that's because I'm sleepy. We only have one eraser so James always says to me 'Don't hog the eraser, Ellen!' Nora got her pictures yesterday. You know what, SHE HAS 75 PEOPLE IN HER CLASS!!!!!*

Satisfied I'd cheered Mother up, I finished by writing in large letters, "I love you! I Miss You! Goodbye. With Love, Ellen." Then I neatly folded my letter and placed it in an envelope.

For the next several days, we cleaned every corner of the house. Sheila, trying to do a good job, decided to vacuum out the closet underneath the stairs where Father had kept his clothes. I was putting away the puzzle on the dining room table when she started to scream. I ran to the closet thinking she'd seen a big rat. But it was only Father's kilt.

In a flash, Aunt Jeanne Marie came up behind me and swooped Sheila up in her arms. She buried her head in Sheila's red hair and whispered in her ear, "Shush, darling, it's okay. Shush, shhh, shhh." But Sheila sobbed and sobbed, just like the day father died.

James flew down the stairs, his eyes frantic. Aunt Jeanne Marie laid Sheila on the sofa and turned to me. "Ellen, please get me a pillow." I grabbed one off the sleeping chair and Aunt Jeanne Marie gently put it under Sheila's head. "James, please grab me a wet cloth, would you?"

Brian walked up and asked, "What happened?"

I shrugged, not really sure what was going on. Aunt Jeanne Marie kept stroking Sheila's hair and telling her everything would be all right. James returned with a wet washcloth.

Aunt Jeanne Marie used the cloth to wipe Sheila's face. Then she wiped the sweat now beading on Sheila's neck. She kept whispering in her ear, telling her everything was all right. Sheila's sobs turned to gentle crying. James could not take his eyes off Aunt Jeanne Marie. He kept staring at her like she might disappear.

After several minutes, Aunt Jeanne Marie caught James's stare. "James, honey, what is it?"

"Nothing," he said.

"Are you okay?"

"Yeah, I'm just watching. I need to learn what to do in situations like these. You know, because you won't always be here."

Aunt Jeanne Marie pulled her lips in, and fought back her tears. Sheila stopped crying and James went back upstairs. Nora and Brian wandered off. I pushed the thought away. I couldn't imagine life without Aunt Jeanne Marie.

On the day of Mother's return, I spent the morning running back and forth to the window, pressing my nose against the glass, looking for the first sign of Grandfather's car. Sometimes I pushed up the heavy frame, pressed my forehead against the screen, and stared as far up Buchanan Street as I could. Looking, waiting. When the car didn't appear, I shut the window and walked away. All morning, my mind couldn't concentrate on anything other than Mother's return. I couldn't wait to see how *normal* felt.

Just after lunch, Sheila begged me to play Parcheesi. We were fighting over who got the yellow pieces when the car pulled to the curb. We both bolted across the living room at the same time. James and Brian came bounding down the stairs and beat us out the front door.

As I jumped off the porch, Grandfather stepped out of the car and opened Grandmother's door. At the same time, the backdoor on the passenger side opened and Mother stood up. I was halfway across the yard when Mother shut the door. After one look at her face, I stopped, unable to move.

An empty, numb feeling came over me as my siblings ran toward the woman who wasn't my mother. The body was the same, the features, everything, but something inside her was missing. The corners of her mouth hung down. Her shoulders slumped. Her eyes, filled with tears, were hollow. The only thing I could think of was, she's dead, she's as dead as my father.

Nora, sobbing, ran and immediately grabbed onto Mother's leg. Sheila started to cry and wrapped her arms around her waist. James put his arms over Sheila and hugged Mother. Brian hung on to a fist of her skirt and sobbed.

But I stood there, unable to move, my legs bound by weights. I kept staring at Mother's blank face, hoping my first impression had been wrong. But it didn't take me long to confirm that when Father died, Mother died too.

A knot the size of a golf ball swelled in my throat. Afraid Mother would think I didn't want her home, I swallowed hard and ran over and put my arms around her waist. But instead of joy, I felt my heart falling down into a deep, dark well. All over again, I hated my father. Only now, I hated him for killing my mother.

And I realized nothing about my family would ever be normal.

I let go of Mother and stepped back. Aunt Jeanne Marie put her arms over Mother's shoulders and locked her fingers behind her neck. For several seconds they stood in the middle of the yard, forehead to forehead, as their shoulders shuddered up and down. Aunt Jeanne Marie bent down and met Mother's gaze. She pulled her close and kissed her gently on the forehead. Then they stood in a tight embrace as if neither one ever wanted to let go. Repeatedly, Aunt Jeanne Marie softly said, "Josephine, darling, I love you."

Arm in arm, Mother and Aunt Jeanne Marie walked into the house, followed by the five of us. Grandmother held the screen door open and said, "Children, be quiet, your grandfather is on the telephone."

Standing at Father's desk with the phone pressed to his ear,

Grandfather was talking, "Yes, she's home," he said. "The children are all crying and I'm crying too."

For the rest of the afternoon, I watched Mother, thinking, hoping, and dreaming that I'd been wrong. Maybe she was just tired. Maybe I needed to give her a few days to get herself together.

But deep in my gut, I knew better.

That afternoon, reality soaked inside my soul. For the first time, I saw how the gun that killed Father also detonated an emotional bomb. That bomb exploded and wounded everyone around us—our family and our neighbors. It stole our innocence. Its explosion imbedded unseen metal in our skin. Metal I'd be plucking out for the rest of my life. I'd forever be finding new pieces in places I never dreamed of. I'd be constantly redressing wounds I thought were healed.

Mother posted bond, and she did come home, but the charges were nolle prossed, not dropped. At any time, if new evidence appeared, the State of Virginia could reassess the case and bring charges against her. In Grandfather's mind, it left Mrs. Lane out there like a slow ticking bomb.

Mother's homecoming was one of those deep, deadly wounds. The kind that never fully heal. The kind you just can't seem to stop picking at. For the rest of my life, I missed that other woman. And I never stopped longing for her to come back, whole.

Her homecoming affected me for years; it shadowed every part of my life. But it never did stop me from longing to be normal.

SPRINGFIELD

MOTHER'S RETURN HOME SHOULD have been the start of my normal life. After all, it didn't take me long to get used to Father's absence. The same thing should have applied to her, especially since the abuse had stopped. And with Aunt Jeanne Marie's help, everything should have fallen right into place.

Within days, Mother went back to work, returning to her job at the *Music Educators Journal*. With her new financial freedom, she brought home our first black and white television. Like starved puppies in front of food, we all lapped up as many hours as possible. And for the first time in my life, I tasted normal as I spread out on the living room floor watching *Mr. Ed*.

Unfortunately, the sweet taste of normal would never last.

Like every summer before, Mother enrolled us all, except James, in the summer recreation program at Claremont Elementary. My new normal life even improved my soccer skills, earning me the coveted position of center. During arts and crafts, I swear, even my macramé and painting improved.

In the evenings, Mother joined the long line of cars circling Claremont to pick us up. Holding tightly to our latest plaster-of-paris statue or our masterpiece paintings, we piled our sweaty bodies in the back of the bus.

At home, we jumped out and went crashing through the front door like little piglets released from a pen. In our playground volume, we yelled for Aunt Jeanne Marie. Aunt Jeanne Marie, refreshed from her afternoon nap, was ready for the onslaught. She took her honorary position on the sofa and gave us her undivided attention. Trying to talk over each other, we rehashed everything, shoving our artwork in her face. When one of us took a breath, someone else jumped in. As always, Aunt

Jeanne Marie laughed in all the right places. Her eyes darted around to each of us. She listened until we all ran out of steam.

After we washed the dinner dishes, took out the trash, and the angels were secure on our bedposts, Mother and Aunt Jeanne Marie talked quietly until well after dark. At night, I lay in bed and listened as their gentle voices floated over me like soft clouds on a clear summer's day.

On the weekends, Mother encouraged Aunt Jeanne Marie to spend time away from the house and us kids. So early on Saturdays, Aunt Jeanne Marie took a city bus into DC and toured the museums and galleries. On those days, as soon as we finished dinner, I paced in front of the house, watching up the street, hoping to be the first to see her heading home.

One Saturday, Sheila decided we should walk to the corner of Buchanan Street and George Mason Drive to meet Aunt Jeanne Marie as soon as she got off the bus. Just before sunset, with Nora and Brian in tow, we started up the street. Brian suggested we surprise her. So we spread out behind the row of forsythia bushes in front of the house on the corner.

After several minutes of crouching behind the shrubs, I gave in and plopped down on the damp ground. The dew had settled, causing the wet on the grass to soak through my shorts. Peeking through the thin shrubs, I followed each car with my eyes as they came up George Mason Drive and whizzed by. I watched as their red taillights grew smaller and smaller before they disappeared over the hill toward Route 7.

When the bus finally came toward us, we peeked over the tops of the bushes and giggled with excitement. Before it came to a complete stop, Aunt Jeanne Marie stood up from her seat toward the back and began to make her way down the aisle. Unable to hold back our enthusiasm, we jumped up, waved our arms frantically, and screamed, "Welcome home Aunt Jeanne Marie," as if she'd been gone for years.

With her arms full of shopping bags, Aunt Jeanne Marie threw back her head and laughed from deep inside her belly.

While still making her way down the aisle, she leaned toward an open window and yelled, "Hello, my darlings!" Everyone on the bus, as if watching a tennis match, turned their heads in unison toward us, then back at her. The door whooshed open and Aunt Jeanne Marie stepped down. While the passengers laughed, we gathered around our beloved aunt, jumping up and down like fans of a famous movie star.

Eager to help, Brian relieved her of a large shopping bag. "What'd ya get us?" he yelled, reaching his little arm deep down inside the bag. In one large swoop, his hand came up over his head, grasping a pair of white satin underpants. The bus revved its engine and pulled away as our audience broke out in uproarious laughter.

All the way down Buchanan Street, Brian waved Aunt Jeanne Marie's panties over his head like a flag.

Aunt Jeanne Marie pulled five large Peppermint Patties out of her purse and handed us each our own. I ripped mine open and took a big long whiff of the sweet smell of chocolate and mint. Slowly, I bit off the edges all around, exposing the white center. Then, wanting it to last forever, I held it between my thumb and forefinger and took small bites. Without chewing, I let each one slowly melt away inside my mouth.

That night, without tossing and turning, I fell right asleep.

I don't know how long Brian had been screaming before his cries jolted me awake. Unsure of what I heard, my feet hit the floor in the sprint position. The overhead light from the boys' room flooded the hallway. I rounded the door and stopped short at the sight of Aunt Jeanne Marie on her knees, leaning over Brian, cradling his head. Sheila lingered in the doorway behind me, her arms folded across her chest. James sat on the bottom bunk next to Aunt Jeanne Marie, his eyes filled with an uncomfortable fear.

Finally, Mother barreled down the hall. Her footsteps pounded heavily on the hardwood floor. Her eyes appeared confused. Gasping for breath, she poked her head in the room and looked around, trying to figure out what was happening. Her mouth hung open and her head bobbed back and forth like one of those loose-headed hula dolls in the back of peoples' cars. Aunt Jeanne Marie, seeing her confusion, softly said, "It's okay Jo, he just had a nightmare."

Mother's face twisted like she'd been punched in the stomach. Her lips closed tight and her head hung down. Her arms fell to her sides and her shoulders drooped. It looked like a hundred-pound weight had been draped over her back.

Still standing in the doorway, she lifted her arm and rested her elbow on the open door. Then she buried her face in the crook of her arm, and cried.

Tears swelled in Aunt Jeanne Marie's eyes. She stood up, and immediately James took her place next to Brian. Aunt Jeanne Marie gently wrapped her arms around Mother. Mother's head dropped and rested on her shoulder. Her cries went from sobs to a gentle whimper.

"Don't worry, Josephine," Aunt Jeanne Marie said, stroking her hair. "It will be all right. I promise, I'll stay with you until your children stop screaming in the night."

Nobody ever told me why Brian screamed that night. And I never thought to ask. By then, I'd pushed the memory of my father so far out of my mind, I didn't think to connect the two. I was too busy trying to grab hold of my new "normal" life.

By September, when we started back to school, Father's death and Mother's hearings no longer made the papers. The other kids in my sixth grade class quit asking questions. I fit right back in with the kids I'd known since the first grade. Then, one night, Mother gathered us around the dining room table. She had an announcement. Even Aunt Jeanne Marie seemed more excited than usual.

"I've rented us a new house in Springfield. It's only twenty minutes from here," she said. "We will move in after the first of the year. It has four bedrooms, a living room, and a den." It sounded like a mansion. We all looked at each other, trying to decide how to respond. Then Mother hit us with the bad news. "Aunt Jeanne Marie has to go home for a few weeks, but she'll be back in time for Christmas and to help us move."

Aunt Jeanne Marie, trying to sound optimistic, explained why she had to leave. "Your Uncle is done with his work in Bogotá and I have to help him pack up our apartment. I'll travel with him to our new assignment in Mexico City. But I promise to come back as soon as we're settled in."

Having never lived anywhere but on Buchanan Street, the thought of a change in neighborhoods sounded exciting. Besides, in Arlington, most people knew how Father died. But in Springfield, I wouldn't have to tell anybody the gory details. The move could be another step toward my normal life.

But how could Aunt Jeanne Marie leave us? The thought made my heart race and the palms of my hands sweat. I wanted to forget about her husband and her life outside of ours. But if she had to be married, then why couldn't Uncle Eugene move to Arlington? Then we could be one big happy family. One big *normal* happy family.

Three weeks later, all Aunt Jeanne Marie's belongings fit back inside her small suitcase. Before noon, the crisp fall air had given in to a hot day. The window air conditioner rattled as it tried its best to cool down the house. Not even the promise of Slurpees excited us as we reluctantly climbed into the VW bus.

Without much fanfare, I joined my brothers and sisters and ordered a cherry Slurpee at the counter of the 7-11 on Columbia Pike. With it freezing my hands, I followed behind everyone across the parking lot to the bus stop in front of the strip mall. Nora and Brian climbed up on the bench, while Sheila and I took turns holding Aunt Jeanne Marie's suitcase. James stood between Mother and Aunt Jeanne Marie as they spoke quietly together.

Several blocks away, the bus began its climb up the hill. Aunt

Jeanne Marie reached for her suitcase and, reluctantly, Sheila let go. By the time the air brakes whooshed, and the door creaked open, every one of us was crying.

Aunt Jeanne Marie put her arms around James and looked down into his eyes and said, "Take care of your Mother." Then she hugged each of us, saying over and over, "I'll be back, I promise."

Sniffling, we lined up on the curb in a row, holding our Slurpees. Aunt Jeanne Marie climbed the few steps onto the bus and made her way down the aisle to an empty seat by the window. She waved and mouthed, "I love you," until the bus pulled away.

Our feet stayed glued to the sidewalk. We stared at the rear end of the bus until it disappeared in the traffic on Columbia Pike. My grief had hit its maximum intensity. Like a rush of water that hits a wall and can go no further, it spread out and settled as we drove home in silence.

Without Aunt Jeanne Marie, Mother struggled to get everything done. At twelve years old, Sheila took over cooking our meals. James tried hard to discipline us, so we wouldn't bother Mother. Brian and I did our best to stay out of everyone's way. We all tried to be Nora's parents, but she fiercely fought us off.

True to her word, three weeks later, we were on our way to Dulles Airport to pick up Aunt Jeanne Marie. Inside the terminal, we ignored Mother's urging to settle down as we raced each other across the massive terrazzo floors. I made a mad dash down a long hallway lined with windows on both sides that gave a better view of the comings and goings of the funny looking transport cars that unloaded passengers. I wanted to be the first one to spot her. The first to welcome her home.

When her tram pulled up, we jumped around wildly while waiting for her to unload. At the first sight of us, Aunt Jeanne Marie laughed out loud and threw open her arms. She got down on her knees and hugged each one of us. To Mother, she said softly, "Josephine, dear, it is so good to see you again." Mother made no effort to hold back the tears as Aunt Jeanne Marie draped her arms over her shoulders and gave her a long hug.

In one large group, we made our way to the escalators and toward the baggage claim. While talking to Mother, Aunt Jeanne Marie pulled five large Peppermint Patties out of her purse and gave one to each of us.

Like before, I slowly unwrapped mine and took a long whiff of the chocolate and mint. In small bites, I nibbled off the edges, and without chewing, let the candy melt away in my mouth.

Then on a cold rainy Saturday in January, the movers pulled up and emptied out the house on Buchanan Street. Leaving behind our dirty walls, the bullet holes in the doorframe, and the stain in the upstairs bedroom, we piled in the bus and Mother backed out of our driveway. Hopefully, never to return.

In Springfield, the new house did feel like a mansion. The foyer was larger than our old bedroom on Buchanan Street. But best of all, we no longer fought each other to get dressed, because the house had two bathrooms.

Few of the boxes were unpacked when I began my first day at Keene Mill Elementary. Wearing my favorite sleeveless yellow sundress with flowers embroidered in pastels across the waist, I sat down amongst a sea of unknown faces. When the teacher finished my introduction, I felt safe knowing the name "Gibson" meant nothing to these kids. When the room fell silent, and all eyes had turned away from me, I let out a deep sigh for having made it past the hardest part.

But after about an hour, the girl sitting beside me leaned over and whispered, "Why are you wearing a summer dress in the winter?"

My face turned red. The teacher's voice faded as I looked the girl up and down. Her grey corduroy skirt fell neatly in folds around her lap. The Peter Pan collar of her neatly pressed blouse folded perfectly over her black cardigan sweater. Even her black and white saddle oxfords looked brand new. Not a scuff in sight. She looked like she had walked out of the pages of the Sears catalog.

As my eyes wandered from my inquisitor, I scoped out all the other kids. Even the boys looked like models. Most wore chinos, with neatly pressed oxford shirts that were tucked behind barely-worn leather belts.

In that moment, the luxury of my new home faded, and the reality of my messy life stepped back into the forefront. I could never tell these kids how my father died. Their lives were too neat and orderly for them to ever understand mine. That day, I felt something new. For the first time, I felt anger toward Mother. Anger that she let me wear a summer dress on a winter day. Anger that she moved us to a town where we clearly didn't fit in.

After a couple months, Aunt Jeanne Marie went home for good to be with Uncle Eugene in Mexico City. Once she left, Mother began to unravel. The stress of keeping a watch on us drove her to quit her job at the *Journal*. Money became tight as she struggled to live off her annuities while picking up freelance graphic design work she did at a light table in our family room. But really, she just withdrew. First from the business world, then from us.

After a few months, Mother took us back to Buchanan Street. The still-vacant house needed to be put up for sale, but we'd never cleaned it out. Dreading the day, I climbed in the back of the bus with the knot in my chest wrapped around my throat.

The duplexes looked smaller and closer together, like little houses lined up on a Monopoly board. At the first sight of our abandoned home, its overgrown grass, and piles of trash littering the side yard, I wanted Mother to drive to the cul-de-sac, turn around, and go right back to Springfield. But she didn't. Like a million times before, she pulled the bus into the driveway, along the two strips of concrete.

A musty mildew smell gagged me when Mother opened the front door. Layers of dirt on the hardwood floor scratched under my sneakers. My foot hit an empty beer can and sent it rattling across the floor. Pieces of trash from when people had broken in were scattered all over the kitchen floor. The whole house smelled like a dirty refrigerator left shut for days in the hot sun. Why would anyone want to come inside our house?

Mother went back to the bus for the mops and buckets. Breathing through my mouth, I ran upstairs to see the bloodstain on the bedroom floor. But before going to the boys' room, I poked my head into my old bedroom. The filthy walls still had two big holes where Father had bolted down our bunk beds. The screens on the windows had come loose at the corners and were flapping in the wind.

When I came back into the hallway, the knot in my chest tightened. A jawbreaker-sized lump clogged my throat. Without any furniture, the walls seemed to creep in, making the rooms seem smaller. Even the bloodstain looked smaller. And it no longer stood out among the other stains we left behind on the floor.

For a split second, I questioned my memory. Maybe the stain had never been that big. Maybe, I never even saw the real blood. Maybe, everything got exaggerated. After all, ever since Mother came home, none of us had talked about the shooting. I could have gotten all the facts wrong.

Then I thought of the door with the drill holes. The last time I saw it, it hung sideways by one hinge with big splinters of wood shredded along the back. But when I entered the doorway of Mother's old room, the door had been removed. Not even the hinge remained. Did vandals take it or did Mother throw it away?

But the door's absence confirmed my memory.

As I made my way down the hall to Mother's bedroom, the smell of soot, like a wet campfire, got stronger. In the middle of the floor, a dozen candles in various stages of meltdown were clumped together in a large circle. They must have been carried around because big globs of wax were spattered across the wood floor.

The thought of strangers hanging out in our house gave me the creeps. And what were they doing with all those candles?

Why would they want to come in here? How could they stand the smell?

Trying to avoid any cleaning, I slowly made my way down the stairs. Ignoring Sheila and Mother's voices in the kitchen, without making any noise, I opened the screen door and held it until it quietly closed behind me. Then I sat down on the front porch to think.

After surveying every room of our old house, and seeing the evidence of the intruders, the house no longer felt like ours. Its essence had passed into another world. A world that, thankfully, no longer involved me.

As I sat there, the bright sunshine did nothing to make Buchanan Street more bearable. After being gone for several months, I no longer recognized many of the cars in our neighbors' driveways. I stretched out my legs and started trying to mentally hurry Mother up so we could go home.

Out of nowhere, a boy about seven years old appeared on the sidewalk. The dried smudges on the bottom of his white tee-shirt matched the gook running out his nose. Staring at me, he shoved his hands deep in the pockets of his blue jeans and shuffled his feet. Shyly, he twisted his shoulders back and forth waiting for me to speak.

As a sixth grader, I no longer felt the need to entertain a kid, so I ignored him. But he wouldn't go away. He just kept staring at me as if waiting for me to explain why I was sitting on the steps of my own house.

Finally, he mustered up some courageous reserve and blurted out like a know-it-all, "You know, a woman shot her husband in that house."

At first I thought, how'd he know that? Then it hit me, he had no idea who I was.

Before I had a chance to answer, without taking a breath, he went on as if proud to have information he thought I didn't know. "Then she buried him underneath the picnic table in the backyard and at night he comes back and haunts the place."

The sentence came to such an abrupt stop it startled me. It took my mind a few seconds to realize what he'd said. Then my imagination went nuts. What if the story were true? I imagined my whole family, on the day of the shooting, standing in the backyard. Mother is calm, but in charge, as she orders us to gather around the picnic table. Brian, Nora and James are on one side, Mother, Sheila, and I on the other. In unison we grunt as we pick up the heavy table and slide it over. Then we all take shovels from the shed and start to dig.

In my mind, the hole was half dug before I looked up and realized the boy had left. Reality and fantasy collided and I began to wonder if he was ever really there. Blood rushed to my face and heated it like I was standing in front of a bonfire. The thought of my family as the gist of a horror story turned my stomach upside down. I could almost hear the symphony of whispers as it spread from kid to kid.

Years later, I was talking with a co-worker as we straightened donuts behind the bakery counter at Giant Food. Having endured hours and hours of therapy, telling the story of my father's death no longer made my teeth chatter. The words flowed easily off my tongue without having to ball my fists to steady my nerves. Even Father's voice came clearly to my head without making me want to silence him.

But this time when I told the story, her eyes opened wide. Not in shock, but in a good sort of way. "My maiden name was Frogle," she said with a smile. "I always wondered what happened to you guys."

What she said next brought back the sick feeling from the day we cleaned the house. "Every kid in the neighborhood thought your house was haunted. They constantly broke in and had séances on the floor where your father died."

Staring at the empty sidewalk where the boy had stood, my anger turned to rage. My Mother didn't deserve this version of the story. She wasn't the murderer they made her out to be. But how do you stop something like this? It would take hours to explain the way my father treated her. To explain about all the guns and abuse. And even if I did tell the stories, they wouldn't convey the crazy look in my father's eyes when he got mad. You'd have to have seen the way he pointed the gun at my mother.

On that day, a new horror took the place of my father's death. The horror of a story out of control, and the fear of what the unknowing can do to the truth.

I also learned you can't control a story. It tells itself from ear to ear, behind closed doors. Like in the game, "telephone," it grows and changes shape. Getting more and more sensational each time.

Defeat tasted bitter on that September afternoon. It lingered on the back of my tongue long after the little boy left. For years, it belched back up when I tried to explain what really happened. But each time I told the story, normal got further and further away. Then, one day, I gave up. I just quit trying to explain the real reason why my Father had to die.

ST. JOSEPH'S VILLA

SURROUNDED BY DISPLAYS of ladies' clothing, I stood inside the front door of Woodward and Lothrop, trying to decide if I really wanted to steal the blouse. I had the shopping bag open and my friend, Sara, standing lookout on her tippy toes over the circular rack. "OK, go ahead," she whispered. Then she gasped, "No, put it back. Uh oh, come on, let's go!" Then she bolted out the door.

Still not sure what she saw, I pushed open the door and got a sniff of the moist summer air, but a firm hand grabbed my upper arm. For a couple seconds, the soles of Sara's sneakers flashed me as she sprinted down the wet pavement in the middle of the outdoor mall. Then her bobbing blond head disappeared into a sea of shoppers.

The man attached to my arm looked like a hunter in his plaid flannel shirt and blue jeans. He had fooled me with his sandy blond beard and ratty-looking long hair. "Come with me. You're under arrest," he said, in his policeman's voice.

My face burned and tears stung my eyes. Still holding on to my elbow, he led me through the lingerie department and down a long hallway in the back of the store. The people passing by cut their eyes toward me, convicting me on the spot. The hunter-policeman opened the door to a small bare-walled office with one metal desk and a grey folding chair. He told me to take a seat, then he left the room.

Several minutes later, a young uniformed police officer came in and sat down on the edge of the desk. Without looking up from his small legal pad, he ran down the litmus test of my name, address, and parent's name. After my interview, he set his clipboard aside, leaned his forearm on his thigh, and rested his chin on the palm of his hand.

Speaking like a concerned teacher, he asked, "So, Ellen, who was the girl with you? Do you know where she went?"

I bit the inside of my lip, fighting back more tears. Not wanting to lie, I said, "I don't know where she went, and I don't want to tell you her name."

"Well, okay, but all we want to do is talk to her. Did she talk you into stealing the blouse? I noticed from what's in your bag that you made a purchase earlier. You didn't come to the mall to steal, did you?"

"No, I didn't." I told the truth. "But she didn't make me do anything, either."

"Well, I'm going to have to take you down to the police station. I'll call your mother and she can come pick you up."

Dread stirred in the pit of my stomach and the back of my throat burned like just before you vomit. Once again, I had done something that would make Mother cry.

It was dark and a light rain had begun to fall when I climbed into the backseat of the police car. Across the empty parking lot, the streetlights reflected off the wet pavement like huge white sparklers. Off in the distance, shoppers, loaded down with bags, walked to their cars. Car doors slammed and engines revved. I stared through the wet window wishing I was any one of them. Anybody but myself.

Sitting in the darkness, with my queasy stomach, I remembered the day I saw Al, sitting alone in the back of the police car. On that day, did he feel as sick as I did now? Did he want to be someone else too? Of all of us, he'd changed the most since Father died. He'd grown up, made good grades, and been the star of his high school football team. Now at the University of Virginia, he came home more often, but he acted too bossy, like he knew what was best for everyone. He acted more like a parent instead of a brother.

Now I thought I might understand him more than I wanted.

In the weeks following my arrest, Mother seemed to distance herself from me. Sometimes we went for days without speaking. But when we did, our conversations quickly turned into arguments.

Then, I got a weird call from Al. Trying to act like a surrogate father, he said he was driving up from Charlottesville to take me out to dinner. But I didn't trust him, especially when I asked if my new boyfriend, Tim, could come along and he said no.

Tim and I had met a few months earlier when I'd spent the night with his sister, Cindy. Two years older than me, he had dropped out of high school and was working construction for a friend's father. On the weekends, he chauffeured Cindy and me any place we wanted to go. When he finally did ask me on a date, I had to let him buy me something new to wear.

On our first date, Tim and I joined the long line outside the Cinema 7 Movie Theater in Bailey's Crossroads to see the new movie, *The Godfather*. We excitedly climbed the stairs to the balcony and sat in the middle of the front row. When the violence started, I covered my eyes and refused to open them for the rest of the film. In the dark, Tim kept asking, "What's the matter?" Fearing he'd think I was strange, I didn't tell him about my childhood.

But now, Al was up to something, and nothing could convince me he had my best interest at heart.

Besides, I still smarted over the way he'd come home the previous summer. His boxes and suitcases had barely hit the floor before he convinced Mother that my room would suit him best. No matter how hard I protested, Mother gave in to Al. I hated the arrogant smirk on his face as he watched me pack up my things and move into Sheila's room.

Now he wanted to take me to dinner. Just the two of us. Perhaps he intended to mend fences. Maybe he finally understood how badly he'd treated me all these years. Maybe this time he wanted us to be friends. Maybe it was a feeble attempt to pay me back all the money he suckered out of me. It might be nice if he acted more like James. I could use another caring older brother.

Friday afternoon came and Al pulled his green and white VW bus into the driveway. Sheila and I ran out to see his new car. Thank goodness it didn't look exactly like our old one, but it did bring back bad memories. I couldn't understand why Al bought it.

When he popped open the side door, I jumped in. His bus had tiny windows along the edge of the roof, giving the interior a brighter, more airy feel than our old one. But it smelled exactly the same. That odd VW mix of burning engine and grease.

Al no longer showed any remnant of the chubby kid who conned me out of my allowance. Now, nearly six feet tall, his strawberry blond hair was cut short. His grey slacks were neatly pressed and his white oxford shirt was tucked smoothly into his trousers.

Nora and Brian meandered outside, walking around the bus. They jumped in and sat down on the middle seat. "It's just like our old one," Brian giggled. "It even smells the same."

"I was just thinking the same thing," I laughed.

Back inside the house, I waited in the foyer while Al and Mother withdrew into her cluttered office. Feeling left out, I went alone into my room and shut the door. Thinking of Al's phone call, I still wondered why he drove all the way from Charlottesville to take me to dinner alone. And if he did come to see me, why was he spending all his time with Mother? Maybe I misunderstood and he planned on taking everyone.

Whatever scam Al had up his sleeve, I wasn't falling for it this time. I'd duck out before dinner and go over to Tim's house.

Mother and Al were seated behind the table at her desk when I entered the room. Mother didn't look up, but stayed hunched over the magazine she was designing. "I'm going to walk over to Tim's house," I informed them instead of asking. Al turned and looked at me like a bossy parent.

"You can't, Ellen. You and I are going to dinner," he said,

like he now ran the whole family. Resenting his intrusion, I wondered what right he had to tell me no.

Ignoring Al, I asked, "Mother, why can't I go?"

Pushing her glasses onto the top of her head, Mother looked up without raising her head. "Alfred has some things he wants to discuss with you. The two of you are going out to dinner." Then she pulled her glasses back down and went back to her magazine.

I stormed out of the room and went into the bathroom and slammed the door. Why did everyone want to run my life? I felt trapped inside my own body. At almost fifteen, I'd convinced myself I'd be better off on my own. At least then I could do whatever I wanted. No more rules, nobody telling me what to do. Sucking in a deep breath, I picked up a brush and looked in the mirror at my frizzy hair. Why couldn't it be straight?

That afternoon, I climbed into the passenger seat of Al's van. "Someone should do something about the nasty smell of these things." I told Al seriously, though he laughed. "It's true," I protested. "No matter what you do, you can't get rid of it. They all smell the same. Even that old bug Father had smelled like this." Al kept laughing at my rant. "It must be the material they use for the seats. And that bumpy texture always leaves marks on the back of your legs. I could spot the design anywhere. Blindfold me and stick me inside here, and I'd know it was a VW."

Al, trying too hard to act mature, broke up my lighthearted fun. "So, Ellen, how are things going at school?"

Cutting my eyes his direction, I stared at him without turning my head. For the past four years, Al had treated me like an intrusion. When he came to visit, he always seemed to have an agenda. Just last summer, he was learning to play guitar and needed someone to sing along with him. Since I was the only one home, he insisted it be me.

Sitting on the edge of *my* bed in the room he just kicked me out of, he ordered me around. Opening a songbook and smoothing the binding flat, he laid it between us on top of the blanket. "You know this song, right?" he said.

I looked down and nodded my head. He began to strum the first bars of the Beatles, "Obladi, Oblada." I tried to sing, but when we came to the chorus, "Obladi, Oblada, life goes on, bra." I couldn't say the word *bra* without thinking of women's underwear. My adolescent sense of humor got the best of me and I burst out laughing.

Unable to see the humor in the song, Al stopped playing, screwed up his face, and snapped, "What's so funny?"

Still chuckling, I said, "Nothing, go ahead, I'll sing." And he started back up. But again, the thought of singing *bra* in a song made me start laughing before we even got to the word. This time Al banged the side of his guitar with the pick, "Ellen! Why can't you just sing the song?"

Giggling, I tried to explain. "I just can't sing the word *bra*. It's such a stupid word to have in a song."

"Just sing it, Ellen," he yelled. "Stop acting so childish." His words cut. James never called me names. Plus, he only got mad at me when I deserved it. And never over silly things. James would have thought it was funny too. But not Al, he never seemed to know how to have fun around us.

When Al pulled the van into the Hot Shoppe's Jr. parking lot in downtown Springfield, it seemed years had passed since Father took us to the one in Arlington. Back then, we always ordered through the speaker from the car. But at this one you had to go inside.

The waitress seated us at a table in the middle of the room. "Order whatever you want, Ellen," he said, like he had turned into a doting rich uncle.

"Don't mind if I do," I replied, closing the menu. Al didn't say a word when I ordered an ice cream waffle.

The waitress took our menus and Al leaned back in his chair and placed his elbows on the armrest. Uncomfortable with the silence between us, I began to chatter in order to give myself time to figure out his angle. I rambled on about gymnastic try-outs and annoying teachers.

By the time the waitress brought our dinner, Al still hadn't mentioned why he'd driven over two hours to take me out to dinner. After our plates were cleared and Al ordered a cup of coffee, he got down to business.

"Ellen, Mother and I have been thinking about your future. We both feel you would benefit from the same type of situation I found at the Richmond Home for Boys."

Whoa, I thought. What is he trying to say?

"There's a home for girls in Richmond, not far from the boys' home. Mother and I checked it out and we think you'd be happy there." He spit the words out so easily, as if discussing which classes I should take the following year.

Key phrases bounced around inside my head, *Mother and I, home for girls, Richmond.* "What are you talking about?" I asked.

"Ellen," Al said. "Listen to me. My time at the boys' home allowed me to find my own way. It gave me focus. If not for the boys' home, I wouldn't be where I am today. Mother and I have discussed it and made an appointment for you to check the place out."

It all hit me at once. So he did have an angle. Here I'd sat, enjoying my dinner, thinking Al might be an okay brother. Only to learn that for the past several weeks, he and Mother were busy concocting a plan to send me away. Mother didn't come up with this on her own. This had to be Al's doing.

"No," I said. "I will not go away. I like my friends here. I have a new boyfriend, and you're not going to take me away from him. Besides, I don't want to live away from home."

As usual, I didn't understand Al. Had he forgotten how Father gave him away to the State? How his absence changed our whole family? For the first time, I considered the possibility that Al had wanted to go away. That maybe he didn't like the rest of us.

Al leaned over and put his arms on the table. He cocked his head and his eyes grew serious. "Ellen, all we're asking you to do is give it a chance. You never know, you might like it. At first I didn't think I'd like the boys' home, but it proved to be the best environment for me."

Then he bit down hard and drew a deep breath through his nose. But I could tell he was mentally counting to ten.

My voice rose slightly. "Look Al, clearly Mother has let her fears for me overtake her better judgment. Everything I do scares her. Every boy I date is potentially abusive. She thinks all they want is sex. And Tim is no exception. She just can't relax and let me grow up."

Al sat still and let me ramble on. Since he didn't respond, I kept going.

"I'm never going to be like Sheila. It's not in me to simply do everything Mother tells me to. I try, but it's hard. To keep her happy, I could never have boyfriends. It's like she doesn't want me to have a good time."

There, I thought. Al, of all people, should understand that.

"Look, Ellen. All you and Mother do is fight. It's not good for you, and it's not good for her. She has too much on her plate with the other kids. You're creating a bad situation for everyone. You need to think of what's best for everyone involved."

I gave up. It was no use trying to convince him of my determination to stay home. He'd made up his mind and helped Mother make up hers. His every move made my blood boil. The way he sat back in his chair like he had life all figured out. The arrogant way he cocked his head to the side when he wanted to make a point. The way he casually folded his hands in his lap while discussing turning my life upside down.

It all made me want to run out the door and jog all the way home. I was sick of other people controlling my life. Al never did care about me. And now he expected me to give up my life for the wellbeing of everyone else. What about what I wanted? Didn't that matter?

Al and I rode back to the house in silence. There wasn't any sense in trying to change his mind. He never listened to me anyway. In one dinner, I'd become a giant roadblock to the wellbeing of my entire family. Back at the house, Mother and Al had another pow-wow without me.

Two weeks later, Mother and I were in the car on our way to Richmond, "just to check the place out."

Classical music played quietly on the radio as the hardwood trees along I-95 zipped by. Scrunched down in the seat, with my eyes blurred, I watched each dotted white line approach and slip underneath the dome of the hood of Mother's new bright red VW bug. For over an hour we rode without saying a word. Deep down, I felt sorry for Mother and the overwhelming burden she had raising us. I longed to be a different kind of kid, one who never caused any trouble. It pained me that since Aunt Jeanne Marie left, Mother just couldn't seem to cope.

But, on the other hand, Mother frustrated me. Aren't parents supposed to know how to handle kids? Aren't they supposed to love them no matter what? I hadn't done half the stuff Al did, so why had she given up on me so fast? Maybe she was the one who wanted me gone. Maybe, like she had with Al, she loved me, but didn't like me anymore.

As she pulled onto the Parham Road exit ramp, Mother tried once again to persuade me. "Ellen, this is really the best thing. If you and I continue the way we've been, we'll no longer be friends. Plus, you've become so difficult, the other kids don't want you around. They need peace too. Even Sheila wants you to leave. Please, look at the Villa with an open mind."

Sheila wanted me gone? Really? My stomach lurched.

We pulled off the main road and drove through two beige brick columns with a crest that said, "St. Joseph's Villa." Immaculate landscaping surrounded us as we came around a corner alongside a row of huge houses made out of the same type of beige bricks.

"Those are the cottages where the girls live," Mother said excitedly. "They're mansions. Only twelve girls live in each one."

That was eleven more girls than I wanted to live with. No matter how nice the place looked, I refused to be impressed.

The smell of honeysuckle flooded through my open window when Mother stopped the car in front of the administration building. Heavy oak trees towered over our heads, putting us in complete shade. Whoever built this place really liked those beige bricks, because this building was made exactly like the cottages and the front columns. We climbed the steps leading up to a large covered porch.

First I decided the people living here must not be very happy, because inside the building someone needed to open some curtains. It took my eyes a while to adjust to the dark lobby. Mother spoke to a nun seated behind a desk, who then ushered us into a large conference room.

I looked around for some windows, but the walls were all made of a dark wood that sucked up the little bit of light coming from the ceiling. About eight empty leather chairs were pulled up to a shiny table without a single scratch on it. Mother and I sat next to each other on one side and waited in silence. After several minutes, a nun walked in wearing a traditional black and white habit. The rustle of her skirt reminded me of those antebellum dresses women wore in the movies.

She introduced herself as Sister Mary Louise. Then she sat and ran down a list of her degrees, all in education. I didn't care, nothing she had to say could make me want to stay.

"Nice to meet you," I said, while wishing she'd go away.

"I understand you're thinking of joining us here at St Joseph's Villa," she said to me, as her eyes searched my face.

With my elbows on the table and my chin resting in the palms of my hands, I stared back, refusing to answer. Besides, I wasn't thinking about it at all.

"I need to ask you some questions." Sister Mary Louise looked down at the pile of papers in front of her. Then she picked up a pencil and began to write.

"Do you have a boyfriend, Ellen?" she said, like we were old friends. Mother turned and looked at me like she didn't know the answer.

"Yes, I do," I answered.

The nun's pencil made scratching noises like a field mouse trying to get through the wall. "Will he be coming to visit you here?"

"He says he will," I replied.

She scribbled some more and went on to the next question without looking up. "Have you ever done drugs?" Then her head pulled up and she stared at me dead in the eye. She'd obviously become skilled at asking this question.

Not sure a lie would convince her, I told a half–truth. "I smoked marijuana once."

Mother's head twitched and she shot a quick glance at me. Clearly, I couldn't take back that information.

Again, without a comment, Sister Mary Louise asked her next question. But all I could think about was, ugh, now Mother knows I tried drugs. Why didn't I lie? Armed with that new information, Mother was certain to send me here to live. I'd sealed my own doom.

Sister Mary Louise spent the remainder of our time explaining the rules. Boyfriends were welcome to show up on the weekends. I could even go on dates as long as I obeyed the curfews. St. Joseph's Villa consisted of several cottages, each with a housemother and a cook. Each cottage housed no more than twelve girls. I was free to roam the compound, ride the horses in the barn, and swim in the Olympic-size indoor pool.

From the outside, it looked like a high-class boarding school, but I didn't want to leave my family and friends. I didn't care how nice the villa was, it wasn't my home. My brothers and sisters didn't live there, and Tim and my friends were two hours away.

Back in the car, the minute I shut the door, Mother began the inquisition. "When did you smoke marijuana? Who gave it to you?"

"It was a long time ago, Mother," I shot back, hoping she'd drop the subject.

"Where did you get it? How did you get it?"

She pulled onto the interstate and tried keeping one eye on the road and the other on my expressions. I didn't want to answer. She kept asking the same questions. Where did I get it and who gave it to me?

Wanting the conversation to end, I said, "Mother, I'm not going to tell you. It was a long time ago."

Mother turned on the radio and, for the next two hours, the classical music created a façade of peace between us.

The minute the car stopped in our driveway, I opened the door, ran in the house, and up the stairs to my room. After slamming the door, I dove face first onto my bed. The heaviness in my heart made each beat reverberate in my brain.

Unable to bear the pressure, I got up and pulled the album, *Abbey Road*, out of its sleeve. I placed it on the spindle, and it dropped onto the turntable and began to spin. I set the needle on the edge and cranked the volume to full. The needle scratched as I crawled back into bed.

The vibration of the music made the walls tremble. The muffled drums and John Lennon's voice sang, "shucht … shucht … Come together …" I turned over on my back and closed my eyes. The steady beat pounded against my chest and the tightness started to fade away.

Two weeks later, Mother and I were back on the road to Richmond. All my clothes fit inside the big orange suitcase Grandmother bought me for Christmas. A small box filled with my records and the new clothes Tim bought me sat on the back seat. My emotions yanked in two directions. One part of me still felt sorry for Mother, sorry that I'd pushed her to this point. The other part boiled with anger that she couldn't handle me. Somewhere in the middle, I struggled to figure out who to blame.

At the villa, I met my housemother, Barbie. With her bouncy blond hair, she looked just like the doll with her name. She helped me unload my stuff and left me alone on my new front porch to watch as Mother's VW disappeared through the front columns. Grateful most of the girls were gone for the summer, I shut the door to my new room.

The springs creaked when I lay down on the narrow unmade bed and stretched out my legs. Putting my hands under my head, I stared up at the tall ceiling. No matter what happens here, I decided, I will not get to know anyone. I will focus on being the best-behaved kid. And doing everything I can to go back home.

That first night, I fell into a deep sleep and forgot where I was. When I awoke the next morning, the voices of children playing underneath the window caught me off guard. I thought of getting up, but couldn't figure out what for. I had nobody to see, nobody to talk to, and no reason to get out of bed. My entire life felt empty. It seemed the whole world was marching along and, suddenly, I disappeared and nobody realized I was gone. In one day, everything that made me Ellen Gibson had been taken away. My home, my friends, and all my brothers and sisters.

A sick lonely feeling wrapped itself around my stomach. Curled up on the bed, I pulled my knees up, trying to keep myself from getting sick. It hurt to think and it hurt to feel. At fifteen, my childhood was over. Longing to control my emotions, I closed my eyes tight and tried to think about Tim. But it felt like a wave had hit me and sucked me out to sea.

With no air conditioning, the cottage quickly heated up. With sweat dripping down my back, I got out of bed and pulled something out of my suitcase to wear. So this is how it works, I thought, you either play by the rules, or you don't get to play. You either make yourself loveable, or people push you away. My life is really up to me, because there's no one else I can depend on.

EPIPHANY

ON THE DAY I RAN AWAY from home, I had no idea I would free Mother's life and mine. Mentally, my own freedom began that first day at Saint Joseph's Villa. Though I didn't know it then, in a small way, I had started to take control of my own destiny.

The change in me came quickly. So much so that, after two months at the Villa, Sister Mary Louise suggested Mother take me home. Instead, she sent James and Sheila down to Richmond to pick me up. Sitting on the backseat, I reaffirmed my intention to be the most agreeable person in the house.

But maintaining my lovable persona proved far more difficult than I imagined. Especially with Mother. While I was gone, she had moved everyone into a three-bedroom apartment closer to the high school. To make room for me, Mother moved out of her room and onto the pullout sofa in the living room. But with the smaller space, it didn't take long for our fights to return, especially when it came to my boyfriend Tim.

I tried to understand Mother's need to protect me, but her fears seemed exaggerated. After all, every man was not like my father.

Then, at seventeen, I got pregnant.

The news didn't bother Tim. I told him on our way to a late dinner at Hot Shoppe's Jr. Ignoring my despair, he did nothing to hide his excitement. While I ate my hamburger, he begged me to marry him.

"No way," I answered, without giving it a second thought. "I'm only seventeen. Besides, I'm never getting married. I'm never going through what my mother did. I might live with someone, but I will never get married. Never!"

A chill went through me just at the thought of tying myself down. It made that old knot rise up in my chest. Just the word marriage made it twist and tighten. Besides, how did Tim know he loved me? We'd only known each other a year. And I wasn't sure if I loved him.

What was love anyway? Father told Mother he loved her. In their wedding pictures, it sure looked like he did. There they are, standing in front of the Little Chapel in the Woods at TSCW. The bright Texas sun bathing them in its finest glory. Her elegant fingers are wrapped through the crook of his arm. The tulle of her long veil is blowing in the wind. She's hanging onto him like he's the golden prize. His shoulders are straight and his square jaw unclenched. They do appear to be quite the happy couple.

If only Mother had seen past his convincing smile. If only she hadn't fallen for his debonair swagger and biting wit. If only she'd listened to her parents.

No, I wasn't taking any chances and ending up where Mother did.

Tim grew silent in spite of my efforts to prod him into talking about something else. Feeling sorry for him, I lowered my voice and said quietly, "Look Tim, I really can't get married. Not to anyone. If we get married, we'll just end up like my parents."

Without finishing his steak, Tim paid the bill and I followed behind him out to his car. Before he started the engine, I said what I'd been dying to say all night.

"I know you won't agree with me, but I'm not going to have this baby. I've already decided to get an abortion. It's only $495, and I think you should pay for it."

Leaving his keys dangling in the ignition, Tim rested his forearms on the steering wheel. For what seemed like hours, he stared at the row of pear trees in front of the car.

Without looking at me, his face twisted. He squinted, making little wrinkles bunch in the corners of his eyes. Ignoring his pain, I turned my head and stared out the passenger window, hoping he'd hurry up and take me home.

"Come on, Ellen," he said, letting out a quiet moan. "I really want this baby. Why can't we just run away and get married? I love you so much and I want to spend the rest of my life with you."

Why did he have to do this? Couldn't he tell I didn't want to feel anything? Nothing for Tim and nothing for the thing growing inside me. I didn't want to even consider any other option except an abortion. And I didn't need Tim's permission. All I needed was his money.

In a last bit of desperation, Tim asked one more time. "Why can't we just have the baby? We can get married. I love you and I don't want you to do this."

But his begging only strengthened my determination. Why did he have to get emotional about something that didn't even exist? After all, it really wasn't a baby yet. Besides, abortions were no big deal now that they were legal. And the clinic didn't even need Mother's permission. It really did seem like the best and cleanest solution.

"I'm doing it, and I'm not changing my mind. I told you, there's no way I'm going to have a baby. I am not ruining my life or anybody else's."

Without wiping his tears, Tim reached down and turned the key. He revved the engine and put his arm over the back of the seat and backed up the car. The chill in his voice stirred up some guilt deep inside my gut. "I'll get you the money, but I don't agree with it, and I think you're dead wrong to do it."

Quickly, I stuffed the guilt back down and began an internal debate. My decision had nothing to do with right or wrong, right? And it had nothing to do with ethics. I really was trying to think of the best solution for everyone. I was doing Tim and the baby a favor. Sparing them the pain of watching me ruin their lives, the way mine was ruined for me.

Anyway, I didn't know if I loved Tim, or if I could love anyone. He had a bad temper and when it flared, I worried he would turn out to be just like my father. With a new determination, I stared straight out the window.

Over the next couple weeks, I told no one, not even Sheila, about my pregnancy. Tim and I had no further discussions about my decision. True to his word, on a bright August Saturday morning, a somber Tim, with his cashier's check made out to Planned Parenthood, picked me up in front of our apartment complex.

During the thirty-minute drive from Springfield to DC, I told Tim my plans to go to college. How I picked out my senior-year classes and hoped to make better grades. He listened, with no response. I just talked to fill the void.

In silence, we entered the building where the elevator took us to the top floor. When the doors opened, we stepped into a long hallway lined on both sides with people sitting in various positions on the floor. Making our way over stretched-out legs, we opened a door to a large, packed waiting room.

Tim walked away from me as I headed for the small sliding glass window where a nurse in scrubs sat. Why couldn't I feel better about my decision? Why couldn't Tim be more like the longhaired hippie who sat casually in a chair by the window? He seemed so at ease chatting away to the girl seated next to him.

While I checked in at the little window, Tim found a vacant seat in the waiting room. Before I had a chance to join him, a nurse called me to the back.

She led me into a small room, with an examination table jutting through the middle. On top, an untouched strip of white paper covered its pale blue leather. Pushing aside a rolling stool, the nurse handed me a hospital gown. "Get completely undressed, including your bra and panties." Then she left, shutting the door behind her.

Several minutes later, she returned, followed by a doctor who looked, in every way, the opposite of Marcus Welby. Young, dark-haired, and impersonal. Without greeting me, he gave the nurse instructions while she helped me put my feet in the stirrups.

Without preparing me for what he intended to do, the doctor began my examination. Maybe he was a good doctor and my discomfort came from having never had a pelvic exam. But either way, he did nothing to soothe my anxiety. Hurriedly, he poked around inside me and shoved my stomach from one side to the other. When he finished, he turned to the nurse, popped off his rubber gloves, and said, "She's too far along, she can't have this procedure." Then he left the room.

A queasy feeling rolled around in my stomach. So, if I was too far along, how pregnant was I?

The nurse, trying to be nice, picked up where the doctor left off. "Don't worry, we can still help you. Get dressed and come into the office next door and I'll go over your options."

After the nurse shut the door, I sat on the edge of the table and swung my feet, suddenly grateful to still have some options. But before I jumped down, a gentle presence entered the room. I didn't see it or hear it, I just felt it. It was that same feeling you get when you don't see them, but you know someone has entered a room. Turning around, I scanned the whole room, but I was all alone.

The doctor's words still lingered in the air. *Too far along for this procedure.* Did that mean whatever was growing in my stomach was no longer a blob, but more like a baby? Was I now carrying a person and not a thing?

A person ... I couldn't get rid of.

As my perspective changed, it felt like God walked across that room and sat down right next to me on the examination table. Almost exactly the way Aunt Jeanne Marie said He would. Somewhere inside my soul, He prodded me to trust Him and let Him help me raise my baby. I sensed His assurance that everything would be all right.

Quickly, I put on my clothes, opened the door, and turned down the empty hallway. The door to the office next to the examination room stood wide open. Behind a large wooden desk, sat the same nurse. When I walked in, she stopped reading and rested her elbows on top of the piles of papers scattered across the desk. Right on top, sat my cashier's check.

"I'm sorry we couldn't help you today," she began. "But you still have options."

"That's okay," I answered. "I think I'm going to go ahead and have my baby anyway."

Acting like she hadn't heard a word I said, the nurse kept talking fast. "If you can get a weekend away from home, we can put you in contact with a clinic in New York that can do the procedure you need. It's simple, really. They inject you with saline, which puts you in labor. Within a few hours you deliver the fetus. After a few more hours, you're free to go home."

So based on what she said, I'd go through everything for a pregnancy, except giving the baby time to grow. I'd go through the worst part, labor and delivery, only to give birth to something dead. Wouldn't it be easier to just let nature take its course? My throat burned. Thank goodness I hadn't had anything to eat.

Like a newly trained salesman giving his first pitch, the nurse kept right on going. "Could you get away for a weekend? Would your parents suspect anything?"

Now frustrated, I blurted out, almost yelling, "I've decided not to have an abortion. I want to keep my baby."

The nurse sat back in her chair and stared at me as if I'd turned into someone else. Taking advantage of the gap in her speech, I spoke up. "I've decided to go through with my pregnancy. My boyfriend's parents are very understanding. They'll help us out. I'll be fine."

She kept looking at me with her mouth hanging open as if her training hadn't prepared her for a response like mine. She seemed disappointed that she'd failed to seal the deal. Admitting defeat, she handed me back my check and mumbled almost under her breath, "You're very fortunate. Most people don't have that kind of support. Good luck to you." But I sensed she didn't have much hope for my success.

Tim didn't see me walk up as he sat slouched over, reading a magazine. I returned so fast, he jumped up, searching my face for clues as to what happened. I blurted out the only explanation I could think of. "I don't know why, but I think God wants us to have this baby."

Tim grabbed my arm and smiled. As if fearing I'd change my mind, he steered me through the crowd of people back toward the elevator doors.

A few weeks later, at our apartment, I helped my brother Jim, who now scowled when we mistakenly called him James, load his few belongings into a U-haul truck. Mother, along with Sheila, Brian, and Nora, piled in Mother's VW bug for the drive down to Charlottesville. In a few weeks, Jim would start classes at the University of Virginia.

I told Mother I didn't want to go. I told Sheila I was pregnant and would be gone when they returned. I made her promise not to tell a soul. She agreed, while trying to conceal her excitement about becoming an aunt.

As soon as the truck pulled away, I loaded my clothes into Tim's blue Chevy Nova. I stuffed my long dirty-blond hair underneath a bandana and we headed off to his sister's in Georgia. Mother and Jim were half way to Charlottesville when we pulled onto Interstate 95. In two weeks, with my forged birth certificate proving I was eighteen, I married Tim.

Back in Virginia, the summer of my senior year—along with my adolescence—passed swiftly into fall. By the middle of October, convinced nobody at West Springfield even noticed my absence, I put high school behind me and prepared for my new life.

The only thing left was to call Mother.

Standing over the phone in Tim's parents' family room, I bit my bottom lip and fought back the tears. Upstairs, someone, probably Tim's mom, banged around in the kitchen, turning the water off and on.

Picking up the receiver, I dialed Mother's number. She answered like a secretary, on the second ring, "Hel-lo, Josephine Gibson speaking."

"Hi, Mother, it's me," I said, surprised by how far away my voice sounded.

The blood inside my head pounded, filling the silence between us. Without giving her a chance to speak I blurted it all out.

"I just wanted to call and let you know I'm okay. I ran away and married Tim. I'm sorry I didn't tell you, but I'm pregnant and I didn't know what else to do."

Even though I expected the sniffles, they still tore a hole in my heart. All my life, I had tried not to cause her any more pain, and yet I couldn't seem to stop it.

"I had a feeling that's what happened," Mother said, without any hint of an *I told you so.*

"You did? If only I'd known, I would have called you sooner."

For the first time with my mother, I felt like an adult. That somehow, my pregnancy had freed her of the burden of raising me. She didn't say it, but I sensed her confidence in me as a mom. I sensed she knew I'd make good choices for my baby. That my baby and I would be all right.

Several months later, alone in my room, I removed the receiving blanket wrapped tightly around my newborn daughter. With her newfound freedom, Kelly stretched her short arms over her head and arched her back. I laid down right next to her as she drew her knees up tight and grunted. She sucked in a long slow breath and held it until her perfectly round face turned beet red.

The scent of the baby powder I sprinkled on her earlier that morning gave me a warm, satisfied feeling. I never thought myself capable of feeling this kind of love. Where did it come from? My insides ached to protect her. To give her a great life. What made me feel I'd throw myself in front of anything that could hurt her?

Staring at Kelly, I thought about Mother. I wondered if seventeen years ago she felt the same protective urges for me. She always said she wanted six kids—three boys and three girls. Our family had been her dream fulfilled.

Then one day I sat in the living room of Mother's apartment and handed her my sleeping baby. Like a pro, she set Kelly on the sofa and unwrapped the blanket that flopped around her. Holding my baby across one arm, Mother smoothed out the blanket and laid her back down. Then she tossed the bottom corner up over her feet and wrapped the sides tightly around her, all without waking her up.

Tenderly, Mother pulled the tight bundle close to her chest and began to rock back and forth. Holding her face close to Kelly's, Mother said something that, to this day, has never left me. "Be careful, Ellen, don't burn yourself out early. You only have so much energy, and when it's gone, you can't get it back."

Taking advantage of her openness, I asked the question that had bothered me all my life, "Why did you stay with Father all those years?"

Mother didn't hesitate, "When I married your father, I took a vow, 'for better or worse,' and I just figured I'd gotten the worse."

"But what about all the abuse? Why didn't you leave then?"

"Your father did move out once. Don't you remember?"

"Yes I do, but why did you take him back?"

"Well, one night, after I pulled into our driveway, your father jumped out from behind the forsythia bushes. He put a gun in my face and said, 'See, I can get you whenever I want.' After that, I figured it was safer living with him where I could keep an eye on him."

Since Mother and I had never discussed Father's death and she so easily offered the information, I decided to ask another question.

"Father wasn't terribly fond of me, was he? I remember being left at home a lot while he took everyone else out."

"I don't think it had anything to do with you," she said. "When you were born, your father was driving a cab full time while getting his Masters degree at SMU. About a month before Christmas, I found out I was pregnant. I was so excited, but I knew we didn't have any money. When I received a small inheritance from a distant aunt, I used it to pay all the medical expenses for your delivery. Then I decided to surprise your father by putting the receipts in a card and giving it to him on Christmas morning. But when he found out where the money came from, he went into a rage. He said, 'Nobody in your family will ever pay for one of my kids.' But I had no way to get the money back. When you were born, he just didn't want anything to do with you."

How sad, I thought. Here Father got her pregnant, and she graciously took care of the bill. Why couldn't he just share in her excitement? Why did he hold it against me my whole life?

To my surprise Mother kept on talking.

"To make matters worse, right after you were born, your father applied for a teaching position at SMU. Without telling your grandfather, he used his name as a reference. When Daddy found out, he called the school and said some unfavorable things about your father. It all ended badly."

So that explained Grandmother's angry letter that "forfeited for all time" any consideration for my father at the time I was born. Did my birth remain a bad taste in his mouth? If it did, then he never gave me a chance.

Mother stopped talking and I became mesmerized watching her with Kelly. For the first time, I caught a glimpse of the kind of mother she'd been before things got out of control. I became the baby in her arms. The one she held tight. The one she put close to her face.

Ten years later, I invited Mother and all my siblings to Thanksgiving dinner at our new home in Manassas, Virginia. While the turkey roasted in the oven, Jim and his wife Pam kept watch over their three toddlers. Sheila and her husband Richard sat in the living room talking to Nora and Brian. While I put the finishing touches on the table, Mother pulled out a chair and sat down.

She looked more tired than usual. Recently, she'd moved to Charlottesville where Jim and Pam had settled. Out of obligation, I called her often, but found it difficult to talk to her. My old childhood desire to fix her life constantly tugged at me. When I did make the trip down to see her, my need to clean her apartment and throw away the piles of newspapers and magazines overwhelmed me. I wanted to take her to a hairdresser and buy her new clothes. But I feared she'd realize how much her appearance embarrassed me.

While I walked around the table straightening the silverware, Mother started to cry. My heart dropped. Rushing to her side, I put my arms around her shoulders and held her tight.

"What's the matter, Mother?" I asked.

Still crying, she shook her head side to side and bit her bottom lip. "It's what I always wanted."

"What? What did you always want?"

"This," she said waving her hand toward the table. "I always wanted all of you to be able to sit down together at the table."

I almost started to laugh. Here I'd spent most of my life thinking of ways to make Mother happy. From early childhood I dreamed of getting rich and giving her a nice house, new clothes, and a fancy car. Yet, I'd never stopped to ask her what she wanted. And to think, I had fulfilled one of her dreams.

That day I decided that, for the rest of my Mother's life, I would focus on loving her unconditionally. Instead of looking at what she had failed to do for me, I would concentrate on what she gave. Sometimes it didn't look like much but, maybe, after her energy got used up, it was everything she had.

For the rest of Mother's life, I made a point to tell her that I thought she did the best she could. That she was a good Mother, and I was proud of her. Every time she responded the same. "I tried Ellen, really I did." But she no longer had to convince me; because I did believe she had given me everything she had to give.

SUICIDE OR NOT?

IN DECEMBER 1974, AL CAME HOME for Christmas. Newly discharged from the Marines, he swung through Virginia on his way to the Paul Hall Center for Maritime Training and Education, in Piney Point, Maryland. His latest educational adventure: to become a Merchant Seaman, just like Father.

Always unable to sit still, after two years at the University of Virginia, Al had dropped out and spent a year backpacking all over Europe. To Mother's shock, he even managed to sneak behind the Iron Curtain and spend a semester in the Soviet Union studying Russian. After he ran out of money, he enlisted in the Marines, hoping to get sent to Vietnam.

But the Marine Corps proved to be more discipline than he craved. When he wasn't accepted to their language school, he left. Now, the life of a seaman beckoned, and he planned to answer its call.

Carrying my ten-month-old baby in her car seat, I banged up the stairs to Mother's apartment. When I got inside, I wasn't surprised to find Nora asleep on the sofa. Obviously, Al had arrived and taken over her room. Several days' worth of *The Washington Post* lay in sections all over the floor. The matted shag carpet needed vacuuming and dirty dishes sat scattered along every surface.

The three-bedroom apartment now seemed larger with just Nora and Brian at home. Since graduating from high school, Sheila had moved into an apartment closer to her job in DC. But, as usual, when Al came home, everyone had to adjust.

Nora rolled over and sat up as I set Kelly's seat on the floor. "I see Al kicked you out of your room," I teased. "Is he up to some of his old tricks?"

"Like hanging me over the balcony until I gave in?"

"Which balcony? That one?" I asked, pointing out the set of French doors.

"Yep, all three stories worth. He held me over the railing by my ankles. Then he wouldn't bring me up until I told him how much I loved him."

It sounded like something Al would do. His cruelty knew no boundaries.

With Kelly in my arms, I banged on the bedroom door until Al muffled a sleepy, "Come in." Sitting up in bed, he squinted and fumbled around, knocking junk off the cluttered nightstand until he found his glasses. Pulling the covers up over his underwear, he sat cross-legged, revealing his tight stomach muscles. What little hair had grown out from his buzz cut was matted and tousled.

Squinting, he blinked hard a few times until his eyes adjusted to the early morning sun creeping in around the shade. Holding his arms out he said, "Let me see her."

Like a man who'd fathered a hundred babies, he took Kelly in his arms and tossed her a few times gently in the air. She giggled and shoved both her fat fists in her mouth. With her legs kicking and arms flailing, Al laid her down on the bed, picked up her little cotton top, and blew a fart noise on her stomach.

"I'm your Uncle Al, Kelly's pal!" he said, laughing along with her. Then he tickled her stomach and started speaking to her in Italian. Kelly's light blue eyes followed every move he made. When he motioned with his arms like the true Italian he wasn't, Kelly cackled and cooed.

Handing her to me, Al, for my benefit, went back to speaking English. "She definitely inherited those good ole Rice looks, didn't she? She's beautiful, Ellen. You know, you should speak foreign languages to her all the time. It would help her later on to learn them. You can't start her out too young."

As usual, Al and I lived in two different worlds. Where did

he think I would learn a foreign language? Didn't he see not all of us lived our lives with no strings attached?

Sliding over a pile of clothes, I sat down on the edge of the bed. No longer feeling the center of attention, Kelly became restless.

Other than a quick phone call from Al to say how "sorry" he was things didn't "work out," at St. Joseph's Villa, the two of us had not spoken about my summer there.

But if I had known this would be the last time I saw or spoke to my brother, our conversation would have been different. I would have told him how St. Joseph's Villa taught me a lot. How it taught me the importance of family, of playing by the rules, and getting along with other people.

But that day, without having an in-depth conversation, Al and I went our separate ways. He became a certified Merchant Seaman and, after graduation, moved to Seattle. There, he enrolled in the Russian studies program at the University of Washington, and between semesters he worked on merchant ships traveling between Seattle and Alaska.

I went on with my life as a wife and mother. In April of 1976, at age nineteen, I gave birth to my son, Daniel. For months, the unfinished conversation with Al bothered me. I thought about writing him a letter to explain my feelings. To tell him I didn't hold it against him for the part he played in sending me away. But I kept putting it off.

Then one day, after a difficult morning getting Daniel down for a nap, Mother called. She dove right in. "I just thought you might be interested to know, Al was found staggering naked along some railroad tracks in Canada." Before I had a chance to ask any questions she started explaining.

"Evidently, he'd been doing some backpacking and must have lost his contacts. You know he can't see a thing without them. Anyway, by the time someone found him, he was incoherent and suffering from exposure. He spent three days in the hospital before coming to enough to identify himself."

It seemed like scary news, but nothing in Mother's voice conveyed concern. Did she fail to see the oddness in the news that Al was naked, roaming along some railroad tracks in Canada?

Silence fell on her end as though she expected a response from me. So I complied. "Where is he now?"

As if she needed my permission to finish her story, she continued. "He's back in Seattle. I talked with him last night and he seems fine."

I wanted to say, "Well okay then, we can all relax. Alfred's fine." Mother treated the news so matter-of-factly, like we were discussing some celebrity gossip. But the story didn't sit well with me. Again, however, the busyness of my life invaded, and my relationship with Al got shoved to a back burner.

Two months later, I was curled up on the sofa with Kelly beside me. As she sucked her thumb and wove the edges of her security blanket between her fingers, I started a new John Le Carre mystery. The air conditioner hummed like it dreaded the impending hot and humid month of August. I remember distinctly that it was the second, because the day before had been Al's twenty-fifth birthday. And all day, I'd thought about him and about writing that letter.

When the phone rang, I didn't expect to hear what Mother had to say. "Al is missing at sea."

"What do you mean by *missing?*"

"It seems he was working on a merchant run from Gore Point, Alaska, back to Seattle. The ship was about five hundred miles off shore when Al became agitated and violent. He got in a fight with another seaman, so the Captain confined him to quarters. After several hours, someone went to check on him but he was gone. They searched the ship, but he was nowhere to be found. They called in the Coast Guard, but after a thirty-minute search they called it off. They said no person could survive that long in those frigid waters."

Thinking it was all a big mistake, I stood silently for a few seconds while Mother started to cry. Knowing she was home alone, I said, "Hang on, Mother, I'll be right over."

I quickly loaded up the kids and drove across town to Mother's apartment. All summer long, she'd been packing for a move back to Texas. With her parents aging, she'd be close by, but not in their backyard. Nora and Brian could finish high school, and the new setting gave her a boost to take another stab at her own graphics design business. Now the start of school was pressing in on her, and she still had a lot of packing to do.

I found her home alone, still in bed, with sections of the newspaper scattered around her. Nora and Brian, probably trying to avoid the situation, had left, for where, Mother didn't know.

Between sobs, Mother raged against the captain of the ship. Thinking out loud, she rattled off all her assumptions. "I just know Al lost his contacts. You know he can't see without them. I'm willing to bet he blindly wandered out on deck and slipped and fell overboard. The ship could have been in rough waters. They said nobody saw him leave his quarters. And nobody saw him on deck after being confined to quarters. If he was in such a bad state, why weren't they watching him more closely?"

The longer she talked, the more it began to sink in that Al was dead. Mother never used the word, and I still held out hope for a better explanation. But reality fell around me like a thick mist. Its moisture invaded every part of me.

Over the next several days, I helped Mother clean up the apartment and finish her packing. Every day, she mumbled on and on about her latest theory on Al's disappearance. She continued to suspect foul play on the part of the ship's crew. But when a representative from the Longshoremen's union called with the results of their investigation, she threatened him with a lawsuit.

Al's death had been labeled a suicide.

"It doesn't make any sense," she said, not particularly at me. "He just graduated from college. He had plans to become a Russian translator. He had to have slipped and fallen overboard. Al did not kill himself!"

As Mother spoke, the image of Al's body, bobbing along in the ocean, got stuck in my mind. It bothered me the Coast Guard couldn't find him. It bothered me to think he felt so alone that he took his own life. It really bothered me that I didn't write that letter.

For the next several days, every morning, I packed up the kids and went back to Mother's apartment. Partly out of fear for her mental state and partly expecting her to tell me what to do next.

But all Mother did was cry and wander around the apartment like a lost child. First she worked in one corner, packing stuff up, sorting it out, then she got distracted and moved to a different area. Then she'd go on a rant about filing a lawsuit to get the *suicide* taken off Al's record.

Everything in me wanted Mother to step up and take charge. Maybe plan a memorial service. Or at least call us all together to share in our grief. But she didn't. When she continued on in her dazed state of mind, I started making excuses for her odd behavior. Perhaps she felt, as long as there was no body, it would never feel like he really died.

About a week after the news of Al's disappearance, I went by the apartment to finish the last bit of cleaning. I no sooner set Daniel down and got Kelly settled, when Mother handed me a letter. "You might want to read this," she said shoving it out to me. Then she walked back to her room and closed the door.

I unfolded the pages and began to read.

Dear Mrs. Gibson,
I don't entirely understand what has happened, but I feel I should try to tell you more about what I know about Al's state of mind recently.

His trip in Canada was a critical point. It marked a culmination of all of his psychic experimentation up un-

til then. He was not crazy, but he had slipped into other probability realms—other worlds—and was completely unaware of his here-and-now physical surroundings ... He was being told—hearing voices—that he was totally worthless, that he'd done nothing but bad all his life, and that he was to suffer eternal retribution. If he kept moving, he'd be all right, but whenever he'd stop to rest a moment, the voices would start up again. He was told that to redeem himself he would have to take a certain test, and that would be to take his life. So he tried. Twice he threw himself into a river, and twice he could not go through with it ... The last time I spoke with him was on the 31st. He then said his plans were to ship out for long enough to make some money, then go to the USSR as a US Information Agency guide for a trade exhibit, and then move to England ... But I think that even then he'd been contemplating the suicide. He took with him very few clothes, and left his guitar here. He seemed even more removed than usual ...

... Somehow we the living must learn from that short life, and continue on. I know I'm much better off for having known that man.

Love, Becki

I plopped down onto my knees and grabbed my stomach. Kelly, sensing something was wrong, cocked her head, waddled over to me, and put her arms around my neck. My head felt full of helium, like it might float off my shoulders.

Brian started banging around in his room. Nora must have still been asleep in hers but, for some reason, I never went to them and discussed Al or the letter. Not once during those first couple weeks do I remember all of us gathering together and talking about Al's death. We each absorbed the grief in our own way by ourselves.

After Mother received Becki's letter, she never disputed Al's suicide. Nor did she acknowledge that he might have taken his own life. And to this day none of us are sure if it was a suicide or not.

But I needed more—some type of closure. If for no reason than to soothe my own guilt. From the first moment, when Father sent Al away, I washed my hands of him. When he came around, I made no effort to treat him like a sibling, like I treated Jim or Sheila.

After he died, we all needed Mother to take the lead. But I now know she couldn't. She just coped the way she always did, by retreating to her room and shutting the rest of us out.

Al's death was never as hard to take as the thought of his suicide. Becki's letter made me feel ten years old again, and helpless. While I'd gone my merry way, accepting my new life as a mom, Al had spent his reliving his failures. And I had a sneaking feeling my trip to St. Joseph's Villa was among the heap.

If I'd only written that letter. Taken the time to say what I'd felt for years. Maybe Al would still be here. Maybe he'd still be, "Uncle Al, Kelly's pal."

EPILOGUE

THE TIRES OF MY CAR RUMBLED over the brick paved threshold as I pulled through the massive iron gates of Quantico National Cemetery. A bundle of six yellow roses, in full bloom, sat on the seat next to me. The sun hung in the sky like a spotlight, highlighting the end of my journey, one that bore down on me with every mile. My body ached with the loneliness of my mother's tragic life.

The grass along the asphalt pavement had just been cut, making each stalk exactly the same height. Its neatness indicative of the Marine Corp she so dearly loved. In front of me, in the middle of a roundabout, high on a pole, a large American Flag flapped fiercely in the wind.

Slowly making my way around the bend, a picture of my mother came to mind. A few years earlier, during a visit from Aunt Jeanne Marie, I had dumped a bag of old photos out on the kitchen table. While I sorted through them, Aunt Jeanne Marie had stood up to refill her cup with coffee.

Turning over the pictures, I sorted them into significant piles. Pictures from Mother's childhood, pictures of us as kids, school pictures. For some reason, the back of one caught my eye. In blue ink, Mother had written, *Josephine Rice, 1st wardrobe after war.*

I flipped it over and there she was, Mother in her finest black and white glory, young and beautiful, stepping out the front door of her parents' Dallas home. The sides of her hair were swept back and neatly tucked underneath a beret. The A-line hem of her skirt came just below her knees. Behind the fitted buttoned-up jacket, a perfectly tied bow flopped down on her chest and a matching coat hung neatly draped over her shoulders.

Aunt Jeanne Marie walked up beside me as I held up the picture. When she leaned in to see what had caught my attention, the steam from her coffee rose and brushed my cheeks.

"Oh, honey," she cooed, pointing at the picture. "When I think of your mother, that's what I see."

That was it, I thought, the moment I'd spent the past several years trying to grasp. The difference between how I saw Mother and how Aunt Jeanne Marie saw her. It was so simple. Aunt Jeanne Marie still saw Mother through the eyes of a little sister. She still saw the piano recitals, the fancy ball gowns, and my mother at her best, in her dress blues. I only saw the broken woman after Father died.

For several hours, we poured over those old pictures, and Mother's other world came alive. I listened as Aunt Jeanne Marie told me how beautifully Mother's long fingers danced across the piano, how gracefully she sat for pictures, how, when dressed up, she looked like she had walked right off the pages of a fashion magazine. I wished I could see my mother like that.

With the memory of that picture fresh in my mind, I pulled the car off the road and onto the grass. I turned off the engine and the intense silence of the cemetery pressed in around me. It had been a while since I had visited her pain.

Leaving my coat in the car, I got out and the cold air whipped through my sweater. When the car door slammed, hundreds of blackbirds fluttered from the treetops. A brisk breeze kicked up, and a sea of dry leaves scampered across the grass like a slew of bugs running from a fire. I leaned into the box filled with regulation vases and pulled one out with a nail in the bottom. It was December 20th, Mother's 73rd birthday.

A gentle sadness crept over me as I wove my way around the other graves toward the back along the tree line, looking for her marker. Additional rows had been added since the last time I visited. But there she was in the middle of the row, my mother, as much a Marine as the hundreds of men buried there.

Standing over her grave, I shoved the vase deep into the

soil and spread the roses out in a circle. With my fingertips, I brushed the dirt off the stone and ripped out the wads of grass that had crept up over the edges. "Happy Birthday, Mother," I murmured. Then I traced my fingers along each carved letter ... *Josephine Rice Gibson, T SGT US Marine Corps. World War II. Korea.*

"Mother," I said, "I'm so glad you're here at Quantico. This is where you belong." Another breeze whipped up and the chill again pierced through me. Not sure what to do next, but not wanting to leave, I stood up, folded my arms across my chest, and looked around.

The desire to really talk to her, to see her sitting across from me drinking a cup of coffee, came over me. I wanted to tell her she changed my life. That I did take all she said to heart. That now, I understood her so much better.

There were so many moments between us never shared.

Instinctively, with my arms still folded, my fists balled up. I swallowed hard and tried to fight back the flood of tears now trickling down my face. My words no longer soothed me as years of emotions churned around inside me.

One more time, I knelt down and placed my hand on the cold marble gravestone. "Mother, I want you to know, I really did love you."

The tears kept coming as I stood up and walked toward my car. Halfway there, I turned around and looked back over the hillside. The six roses were the only flowers on the sea of flat gravestones spread across the large field. Down the road, off in the distance, the American flag still blew in the wind.

The scene reminded me of the letter she wrote home to her parents from Cherry Point. How she sat alone in her room, reflecting on a great day. She'd just gotten ready for bed after watching the nightly lowering of the flag. The ceremony had moved her as she described it in detail.

"I am happy here, I am happy to the very core of me."

Steering my car onto the freeway with my head high and my

shoulders back, I said, feeling as though she heard me, "Mother, I think you did the best you could. I want you to know, I'm proud of you for being a Marine. I'm really proud to be a Texan just like you. But, most of all, I'm just proud to be your daughter."

Pushing a CD into the slot, I advanced the tracks to the last one and turned up the volume. A solo pianist began playing the first bars of *Pathetique*. As the familiar notes played, I saw her sitting at the piano in our old house on Buchanan Street. The long fingers of her left hand are stretched wide, playing multiple keys. The fingers of her right are arched as they plink out the higher notes. I'm there too, standing right next to her, holding the corner of the page, watching each note.

The pace picks up and I continue following along. But when Mother looks my way and nods, her eyes are tender, and in them I see it is time to turn the page.

So, I do.

Dear Friends,
If after reading this book you too feel the nudge of God to be truly transformed by Him, to become different, not perfect, but changed, I invite you to pray this prayer.
In His Love,
Ellen

"Jesus, I do believe you are the Son of God and that you died on the cross to pay the penalty for my sin. Forgive me. I turn away from my sin and choose to live a life that pleases you. Enter my life as my Savior and Lord. I want to follow you and make you the leader of my life. Thank you for your gift of eternal life and for the Holy Spirit, who has now come to live in me. I ask this in your name. Amen."

After praying, please affirm your decision with a friend.

"And this is what God has testified: He has given us eternal life, and this life is in his Son. Whoever has the Son has life; whoever does not have the Son does not have life. I have written this to you who believe in the name of the Son of God, so that you may know you have eternal life."
1 John 5:11-13

Acknowledgements

Thanks to Susie May Warren, Eva Marie Everson, and Jessica Everson for such tender hearted editing. As all good editors do, they made me a better writer. To my agent Chip MacGregor, whose heart is so big he takes on little writers like me, just because he believes in us. To my children, Kelly Negvesky and Daniel Gee, who in spite of their parent's dysfunction, managed to love us deeply, then go on and pour their hearts into families of their own. I'm so proud of you both. A deep thanks to my sister Sheila, my dearest friend and confidant. Your constant support has held me through every single challenge of my life. And thanks to my brother Jim, my father figure, my mentor, editor, friend. You have always been so much more than a brother to us all.

But most of all, thanks to my husband Tim. For always believing in my writing. For keeping me stocked with the best computers and word processors—starting with that bizarre Commodore 64. I will never stop missing you.

Made in the USA
Columbia, SC
15 October 2017